Leemei Tan

Lemongrass
and
Ginger

COOKBOOK

Vibrant Asian recipes

DUNCAN BAIRD PUBLISHERS

LONDON

DEDICATION
**This book is dedicated to my family,
Arnaud, Nelly, Azma and Kristin.**

LEMONGRASS AND GINGER COOKBOOK
Leemei Tan

Distributed in the USA and Canada by
Sterling Publishing Co., Inc.
387 Park Avenue South
New York, NY 10016-8810

First published in the United Kingdom
and USA in 2012 by
Duncan Baird Publishers Ltd
Sixth Floor, Castle House, 75–76 Wells Street
London W1T 3QH

Managing Editor: Grace Cheetham
Editors: Camilla Davis and Josephine Bonde
Art Director and Designer: Manisha Patel
Production: Uzma Taj
Americanizers: Constance Novis and Jan Cutler
Commissioned Photography: Yuki Sugiura
Food Stylist: Aya Nishimura
Prop Stylist: Wei Tang

Library of Congress Cataloging-in-Publication
Data available

ISBN: 978-1-84899-013-5

10 9 8 7 6 5 4 3 2 1

Typeset in Arno Pro and Questal
Color reproduction by Colourscan, Singapore
Printed in China by Imago

For information about custom editions, special sales,
premium and corporate purchases, please contact
Sterling Special Sales Department at 800-805-5489 or
specialsales@sterlingpub.com

PUBLISHER'S NOTE:
While every care has been taken in compiling the
recipes for this book, Duncan Baird Publishers, or any
other persons who have been involved in working on
this publication, cannot accept responsibility for any
errors or omissions, inadvertent or not, that may be
found in the recipes or text, nor for any problems that
may arise as a result of preparing one of these recipes.
It is important that you consult a medical professional
before following any of the recipes or information
contained in this book if you have any special dietary
requirements or medical conditions. Ill or elderly people,
babies, young children and women who are pregnant or
breastfeeding should avoid recipes containing raw meat,
raw fish or uncooked eggs.

NOTES ON THE RECIPES:
Unless otherwise stated:
All recipes serve 4
Use large eggs and medium fruit and vegetables
Use fresh ingredients, including herbs and chilies
1 tsp. = 5ml   1 tbsp. = 15ml   1 cup = 240ml

contents

INTRODUCTION

Home for me is Kedah in the northwestern state of Peninsula Malaysia where I grew up with my mom, dad, big sister and little brother. Picturesque, complete with lush paddy fields and dotted with kampungs (villages), the Kedah region is the "Rice Bowl of Malaysia," producing more than half of Malaysia's rice supply.

Malaysia is a society where many diverse food cultures mix so, as I grew up, not only did I have the opportunity to eat many different foods but I was also encouraged by my parents to be bold and adventurous with what I ate. Delicious foods of all kinds were available to us in abundance, and right on our doorstep.

I grew up in a town where the main street was lined on both sides with a collection of stores and homes, and this is where we lived. Dad ran his retail business downstairs, we lived upstairs, and in our large backyard my mom grew chili bushes, pandan plants and mango, papaya and calamansi (a type of citrus fruit) trees. We also raised free-range chickens.

Serving fresh, healthy and delicious meals to her family was important to my mom, and each day after we left for school she would make her way to the nearby markets to source the freshest ingredients to use when cooking our dinner. Because Friday was the first day of the weekend in Kedah State it meant I could join Mom at the markets. After what seemed like years of nagging her to let me come along, my first outing to the markets was a real adventure. One hand clinging onto my small straw bag and the other holding onto Mom's hand, I was mesmerized by the sounds, sights and smells: traders and farmers vying for each customer's business; displays of amazing fresh fruits and vegetables; and massive boxes of crushed ice covering fresh seafood and fish shipped in daily from the two main shipping ports—Kuala Perlis and Kuala Kedah. I found it captivating, but equally as exciting for me was watching Mom turn all the wonderful fresh produce into amazing food. It was never a chore for me to get involved in the kitchen; I was a willing volunteer, taking on any task Mom felt confident I could cope with.

MOM'S LITTLE HELPER

Those early years in the kitchen—learning about different fresh roots, spices and other important ingredients in an Asian kitchen; helping with the chopping, grinding, pounding and slicing; and watching my Mom gutting fish and preparing fresh poultry before cooking—are all experiences that have definitely formed my appreciation of fresh produce and my love of creating new dishes. Food was such an important part of my upbringing, but it wasn't until quite a few years later that I understood just how priceless this time was. Even though I was a very willing helper, there were times when I complained about how the tasks given to me were all related to food preparation: "Why can't I cook a dish?", I would ask. The response was always the same, "You have plenty to learn before I let you handle the wok." I would pull a long and sulky face, not realizing that Mom wanted me to have a solid base in cooking. Back then, I could only observe how to do proper stir-frying, braising and steaming, but now I realize just how clever and insightful she was.

MY FORMATIVE YEARS

After I finished high school, I went to a college in Kuala Lumpur. During this time, eating out became part of my lifestyle. There were street-food hawkers almost at every corner, and it didn't take me long to get enthusiastic about the food scene. I used to eat regularly at restaurants, so I tasted many different cuisines from around the world, further fueling my interest in food. But there is something quite special about home cooking, and I had always been pampered with Mom's. Luckily for me I had a wonderful landlady who was both kind and a very good cook. Mrs. Seow often spoiled me with her home cooking. I will always remember fondly how on hot, humid days she would treat me to a traditional soupy dessert to help cool me down. Another lip-smacking dish that she prepared often was Claypot Chicken Rice (*see page 88*), which appeared to be so simple yet was flavorsome. Her secret was to use a free-range chicken and to be bold with seasoning.

From Kuala Lumpur I moved to Perth, Australia, for two years to complete my university degree. Leaving my home and my family was hard, but I was embarking on a new adventure and I was with a group of university friends. This period of time turned out to be one of those important milestones in my life—it was also where my cooking skills were put to the test.

I shared a house with three friends: Peh-Ling, who was not confident in her cooking skills (she was in charge of chopping the vegetables); Huey-Mein, who cooked a little (but everything looked dark and tasted sweet, as she is very fond of dark and sweet soy sauce); and there was Cathy, who like me had had a lot more hands-on experience in the kitchen. It was Cathy and I who ended up cooking most of the time.

As in my parents' house, we would always sit down to a bowl of fluffy white rice, which we would eat with a few different meat, fish and vegetable dishes. All nicely presented at the center of the table, the food was fresh and simple, fragrant and warm, delicious and healthy. I have many fond memories of this time, and quite recently Cathy and I were reminiscing about our mealtime moments when she suddenly paused and exclaimed, "Never once did it cross anyone's mind to start dinner without everyone being home!" It was our home away from home, a house filled with warmth and laughter. During those few years, cooking without any guidance from Mom, I learned to improvise, and this made me a keener and more confident cook.

LIVING IN LONDON

From Perth I returned to Kuala Lumpur to work, then, about seven years ago, I decided to take a sabbatical and pursue my dream to travel and experience more of the amazing world we live in. I headed for London, where I'm still based. My first year in London flew by. I cooked more than I used to back in Malaysia, and my weekly telephone conversations with Mom were never without a discussion of food of some kind. There was also lots of "How do you…?", "Do you remember that dish that you made…?" and "You know the spice paste that was freshly ground, how much of each ingredient do I use?" It was during this year that I realized just how much I had taken for granted during the cooking sessions in my parents' kitchen, and just how infectious Mom's enthusiasm had been!

It was during my second year in London, after I met Arnaud, who is now my fiancé, that the next stage of my food journey started. Along with our shared passion for food, we both love traveling and, Arnaud being French, meant we made many trips to France. Slowly I was introduced to a different style of cooking from the many different regions of France, and new and amazing ingredients that were so different from those we use in Malaysia.

Arnaud's mother, Nelly, also loves cooking and enjoys good food, and for her, as it is for me, cooking is relaxing, therapeutic and never a chore. When I first met Nelly, I didn't speak French or she Mandarin or English, and it was food that helped us to connect with each other. Nelly, like my mom, is one of the best role models. Her impeccable skills inspire me, and I love her home cooking. It was meeting Arnaud and then Nelly that got me wondering, "Is working with food my destiny?"

Traveling with Arnaud to the different regions in France and to many different countries—experiencing the wonderful cultural diversities and different styles of cooking—has greatly influenced my own cooking. From each place I visit, I come away with a handful of classic recipes and a new appreciation of what authentic cooking means. This has inspired me to learn new cooking techniques and to develop my cooking style with an increasingly more international and modern flavor.

One life-changing experience was my visit to Tsukiji fish market in Tokyo, which gave me an insight into the importance of eating top-quality, fresh ingredients and preparing food simply. When you cook with fresh produce, you can turn a good dish into something that is exceptionally tasty, even when using the simplest cooking techniques. Nothing is more amazing than eating the freshest tuna sashimi that, sliced in a particular way, practically melts in your mouth. Even eating a freshly-made bowl of the humble soba noodles can bring about beaming, satisfied faces. At Tsujiki fish market, and generally when traveling through Japan, I learned so much about the importance of the words "practical, simple, healthy and delicious" when it comes to cooking and food. And this is now central to my style of cooking. A great example of this is my Soy & Mirin Tuna on Soba Noodles (*see page 30*).

Simplicity lets the food speak for itself. If I am ever asked what was the most memorable dish I ate when traveling somewhere specific, my answer seems always to be something that was prepared in home-cooking style— simply presented yet bursting with flavor. And when I get home and recreate these dishes in my own kitchen, I get great satisfaction from this approach.

I remember a particular experience when I was in Vietnam, which instilled in me, and reassured me, that in the kitchen patience is a virtue. (And now I pay even more attention to how soup stock tastes and looks.) I watched an amazing lady in her sixties start her day at 4 A.M. to prepare the stock for her version of Vietnamese Chicken Noodle Soup (*see page 144*) that she later sold on her food stand. Onions and ginger were toasted until slightly charred before adding them to the water, along with star anise, cinnamon sticks, cloves and chicken carcasses, to make a fresh, rich stock. Over the lowest heat possible, she left the ingredients to simmer ever so gently for hours, so as to avoid any cloudiness. The result was the most delicious, deep and flavorsome stock, with a hint of licorice, cloves, onions and ginger. That, for me, is the result of patience and passion in cooking, which then brings warmth and happiness to those people who get to enjoy the meal.

Traveling has given me the incredible opportunity to immerse myself in learning about local foods and a country's culture. I have had many fantastic and special experiences when I spent time really talking with local people to understand their culture, which, especially in Asian countries, has often evolved through food and, in particular, spice trading.

These conversations and observations have made me understand just how important, if not essential, it is to preserve the authenticity of recipes however much you adapt and modernize them. And this realization was in part the impetus behind starting my food and travel blog, My Cooking Hut. I wanted to do my bit to spread the love of food, and its heritage, to other people all around the world.

MY COOKING HUT

For me, my blog is not only a way to record my food and travel experiences, but also a way to share and reminisce with fellow food and travel enthusiasts. Food is a wonderful way to bond people together, and through the world of blogging I have connected with so many fantastic, like-minded people from many different cultures and parts of the world.

It may only be a small contribution, but I hope that sharing my passion, knowledge and skills will inspire an interest in food and the origin of different dishes in people of all ages. I hope it helps them appreciate just how closely related food and lifestyle are.

Stepping into the food-blogging world may not have been planned, but it has given me a better insight into many different cuisines and it has allowed me to explore my own talents and interests. Writing and talking about food led me to food photography and styling. Never before had I appreciated the potential I showed in these areas, and as each day passes and I further submerge myself in my blog work, my passion grows stronger. Photography has enabled me to look at things differently and capture not only the beauty of food but to appreciate some of the amazing scenery that God has blessed our world with.

What keeps me going is the encouragement that I receive from the loyal readers of my blog. Every day I am touched by the sweet and kind words I receive. I am so thankful for them, and it is this appreciation that makes me even more determined to produce and share beautiful recipes and photography.

LEMONGRASS & GINGER

Writing the recipes for this book, remembering all the people and places that have inspired me and reflecting on just how far my food journey has taken me since that first trip to the market with Mom, has been, if truth be told, almost unbelievable. As I've sat in front of my computer screen typing away, so many vivid images have popped back into my mind that I can almost smell and taste the food, hear the banter and laughter, and feel the joy of sharing these moments with friends, family and new-found, food-loving enthusiasts. Being able to bring these experiences to life in my kitchen, and now in this book for you to cook and enjoy, is incredibly rewarding; to have this opportunity to show you just how tasty, rich and flavorsome authentic Asian cooking is, and how easy it is to prepare at home.

The recipes in this book are my take on the wonderful, classic recipes of Southeast Asia. Many of them use modern ingredients and equipment, and different, more approachable techniques. They include recipes for dishes I have tasted during my travels that stand out in my memory. There are some that have been handed down from my family and others that are recipes that were inspired by meals I enjoyed with people I've met or have eaten with family and friends.

As you flip through the book and read the recipes, you will discover, as I have, the significant differences in dishes from one country to the next, despite the countries bordering one another, such as China and India. Or, even though two countries are far apart, there can be incredible similarities between the ingredients and spices, as in Malaysian and Indian cuisines. There are so many different types of delicious Asian foods with incredible flavors and wonderful ranges of tastes, and the recipes I've included within each chapter have been chosen specifically so you can experience the diversity of Asian food.

When writing and compiling the recipes, it was important to me that they accurately reflect the flavors and nuances of the different countries, and to do this, a lot of fresh spices are used. Within the Basics section of the book you will find 20 spice pastes (*see pages 206 to 210*) that are so easy to make, you will never again need to buy the ready-made versions. Using either a food processor or mortar and pestle, you can grind up fresh spice pastes in just a few minutes. Each paste recipe makes enough for one recipe or a meal for four people, but can easily be doubled, tripled, etc., and can also be stored in the refrigerator for up to one week.

No matter which Asian cuisine you are cooking, the balance of flavors is very important. There is no secret to making the most perfect and tastiest dish—it all lies in the tasting and balancing of flavors. So, when cooking my recipes, or if you are taking inspiration from them to create your own, taste, taste and taste again while you are cooking. This is an important Asian cooking technique that I guarantee will help you to achieve a harmony of flavors in every dish you cook.

Another important tip, as mentioned before, is to use the freshest ingredients possible. And if you have a well-stocked storecupboard, with all the condiments that are essential for Asian cooking, such as light soy sauce, dark soy sauce, sweet soy sauce, fish sauce, Chinese rice wine, cooking sake, mirin and sesame oil, you can create healthy and tasty Asian food at home with ease.

I live to eat, and love to eat, and I know this will never change. I hope when you are reading and using my book you will be inspired, and that I manage to set off a similar passion for good, fresh food in you.

JAPAN & KOREA

In contrast to the spiciness of Korean and other Asian foods, Japanese cuisine is mild in flavor, with sweetness and saltiness as the key tastes. It is simple, light and elegant, and is cooked using the best-quality, freshest ingredients available. Japanese cooking emphasizes the purity of the natural ingredient and eating seasonally. Key ingredients used are: shoyu, Japanese soy sauce; mirin, a sweetened sake; rice wine vinegar; and miso, a fermented bean paste, which is an ingredient used to make Japanese stock. Rice is also an important part of Japanese meals, and is the base ingredient of many popular dishes, including Sea Bream Nigirizushi (*see page* 25) and Tempura Shrimp Temaki (*see page 29*).

Korean dishes are largely based on rice and noodles and, because of the liberal use of Korean hot red chili pepper and hot pepper paste, are very much associated with piquancy. Other key ingredients used in Korean cooking are soy sauce, garlic, ginger, scallions, sesame oil and toasted sesame seeds, and nearly all meals are served with kimchi, a Korean condiment most commonly made with cabbage. I use Bok Choy Kimchi (*see page 36*) as a nice variation on the classic. There is an abundance of seafood in Korean cooking. Pork and chicken are often eaten as well, but beef is by far the most popular meat, and is used in dishes such as Bibimbap (*see page 22*) and Sesame Barbecued Beef (*see page 24*).

chicken teriyaki & onigiri bento

Delicious, healthy and convenient is how I describe a bento, a simple lunch in a box that consists of vegetables, meat or fish, and rice. There are many variations of bento, and you can include anything you like—not just what I've selected here.

SERVES 4
PREPARATION TIME 25 minutes, plus 25 minutes marinating time
COOKING TIME 15 to 20 minutes, plus cooking the rice

scant ⅔ cup mirin
scant ½ cup shoyu
2 tablespoons sake
2 tablespoons sugar
½-inch piece of ginger-root, peeled and finely grated, juice only, pulp discarded
4 chicken legs, skin on and deboned (*see page 215*)
1 tablespoon sesame seeds
½ recipe quantity Boiled Short-Grain Rice (*see page 214*)
14 ounces baby spinach leaves
1 tablespoon sunflower oil
9 ounces tomatoes
sea salt

1 Put the mirin, shoyu, sake, sugar and ginger juice in a bowl. Mix until the sugar is dissolved, then add the chicken legs and coat well in the liquid. Cover with plastic wrap and leave to marinate in the refrigerator about 25 minutes.

2 Meanwhile, heat a skillet over medium-high heat, then add the sesame seeds and dry-fry and follow a few minutes until the seeds begin to pop. Tip onto a plate and set aside.

3 Divide the warm, boiled rice into 8 equal portions. Moisten your hands to stop the rice from sticking to them and scoop up a portion of rice. Shape it into a ball, then slightly flatten and sprinkle with the toasted sesame seeds. Repeat with the remaining portions of rice and set aside.

4 Bring a saucepan of salted water to a boil, add the spinach and cook about 30 seconds. Drain and refresh the spinach under cold running water. Squeeze out any excess liquid and pat dry with paper towels. Divide into 4 equal portions, then shape each portion into 3 small balls. Set aside.

5 Heat the oil in a large saucepan over medium-high heat. Add the chicken pieces, skin-side down, and cook and follow 5 to 6 minutes on each side until golden brown and cooked through. Pour in the marinade and bring to a boil a few seconds, then reduce the heat to medium. Continue to cook until the sauce starts to thicken.

6 Remove the pan from the heat and cut the chicken into bite-size slices. To assemble, divide the rice portions, spinach balls, chicken and cherry tomatoes into each bento or lunch box.

korean fried chicken

A few years ago in New York, I stopped by a popular Korean eatery that is most famous for one dish—Double-Fried Chicken. That doesn't sound so sensational, right? I took my first bite from the chicken wing and was left speechless. Really crispy skin glazed with a soy sauce mixture. Amazing! I just wanted to keep eating and eating. Here I've recreated the recipe with the addition of sesame seeds for extra crunch.

SERVES 4
PREPARATION TIME 20 minutes
COOKING TIME about 1 hour

heaping ¾ cup all-purpose
  flour, plus extra for dusting
3 tablespoons cornstarch
4 tablespoons light soy sauce
1 tablespoon sugar
2 tablespoons honey
1 tablespoon sesame oil
4 garlic cloves, finely chopped
½-inch piece of ginger-root,
  peeled and finely chopped
2 tablespoons sesame seeds
2 cups sunflower oil,
  for deep-frying
2 pounds 4 ounces
  chicken wings

TO SERVE
1 recipe quantity Boiled
  Long-Grain Rice (*see page
  214*)

1 Sift the flour and cornstarch into a bowl, then gradually mix in scant 1 cup water to form a batter and set aside.

2 In a small saucepan over medium-high heat, add the soy sauce, sugar, honey, sesame oil, garlic, ginger and 1 tablespoon water. Bring to a gentle boil, then reduce the heat to low and simmer 10 minutes and follow until the mixture starts to thicken. Remove from the heat, strain over a large bowl and set aside.

3 Meanwhile, heat a skillet over medium-high heat. Add the sesame seeds and dry-fry a few minutes until the seeds begin to pop. Tip onto a plate and set aside.

4 Heat the sunflower oil in a deep, heavy-bottomed saucepan to 350°F, until a small piece of bread dropped into the hot oil turns brown in 15 seconds. Lightly dust the chicken wings with flour, then coat with the batter and gently slide into the oil. Working in 2 or 3 batches, fry the wings 10 to 15 minutes per batch until lightly golden brown. Remove from the oil, using a slotted spoon, and drain on paper towels. Avoid overcrowding the saucepan because this will lower the temperature of the oil.

5 Let the chicken wings cool 5 minutes and bring the heat back to 350°F. Working in batches, refry the chicken 2 minutes longer per batch, or until golden brown and crisp. Remove from the oil and drain well on paper towels. Put the chicken pieces in the large bowl with the soy sauce mixture and toss until well coated. Sprinkle with the toasted sesame seeds before serving warm with boiled rice.

japanese pork & cabbage pancakes

Osaka in Japan is a heaven for food lovers, and when you stroll around its recognized area of gastronomy, Dotonburi, you are spoiled for choice. Restaurants line both sides of the streets. One of the specialties from Osaka is Okonomiyaki, a savory pancake cooked on a cast-iron grillpan and topped with a sauce much like Worcestershire sauce, along with mayonnaise and bonito. It is also very popular in the area of Hiroshima but there, instead of mixing all the ingredients into the batter, Hiroshima-style Okonomiyaki is prepared by layering the ingredients.

MAKES 8 pancakes
PREPARATION TIME 25 minutes
COOKING TIME about 1 hour
20 minutes

heaping 1¾ cups all-purpose
 flour
½ teaspoon sea salt
1 tablespoon sake
1 tablespoon mirin
½ small white cabbage, core
 removed, rinsed and finely
 chopped
5½ ounces ground pork
5½ ounces raw, peeled jumbo
 shrimp, deveined and cut
 into small pieces (*see
 page 216*)
2 scallions, finely chopped
2 eggs, at room temperature
sunflower oil, for greasing
light mayonnaise, to serve
bonito flakes, to serve
 (optional)

SAUCE
3 tablespoons tomato ketchup
4 tablespoons Worcestershire
 sauce
2 teaspoons light corn syrup
2 teaspoons shoyu

1 To make the sauce, put the ketchup, Worcestershire sauce, light corn syrup and shoyu in a small saucepan over medium-high heat. Stir well and cook 2 to 3 minutes until the sauce starts to thicken. Set aside to cool.

2 Sift the flour into a large mixing bowl, add scant 1 cup water and mix well to form a thick batter. Stir in the salt, sake and mirin, then add the cabbage, pork, shrimp and scallions. Break in the eggs, mix until well combined, and set aside.

3 Pour some oil into a large, heavy-bottomed skillet over medium-high heat, then use a piece of paper towel to grease the pan evenly and soak up any excess oil. When the pan is hot, add 3 or 4 tablespoons of the mixture and flatten it into a 4½-inch disk. Cook 8 to 10 minutes, then, using a spatula, flip the okonomiyaki over and cook the other side 8 to 10 minutes, or until golden brown and crisp. Remove from the pan and keep warm while you make the remaining pancakes. If they will fit in the pan, cook 2 okonomiyaki at a time. Oil the pan again as required.

4 Divide the Okonomiyaki into individual serving plates, brush with the sauce and then top with a generous dollop of mayonnaise. Sprinkle with bonito flakes, if using, and serve warm.

japanese beef stew

The Japanese absolutely love to eat beef cooked in hotpot-style. The beef is very thinly sliced, stir-fried and then simmered with vegetables in a flavorful dashi. Here I suggest using boneless beef top round steak or sirloin steak. However, for a truly sensational dish you could use wagyu beef. Originating in Japan, wagyu is now available worldwide. The fat is evenly distributed throughout the flesh and melts as the meat is cooked, giving it a soft and juicy texture and a rich flavor.

SERVES 4 to 6
PREPARATION TIME 20 minutes, plus making the Dashi
COOKING TIME 45 minutes

2¾ ounces sugar snap peas
1 tablespoon sunflower oil
1 pound 2 ounces boneless beef top round steak or sirloin steak, fat trimmed, cut into bite-size pieces
1 onion, cut into wedges
3 carrots, cut into bite-size pieces
2 potatoes, quartered
1 parsnip, cut into bite-size pieces
9 ounces daikon radish, quartered
½ recipe quantity Dashi (*see page 211*)
2 tablespoons sake or rice wine
2 tablespoons sugar
4 tablespoons shoyu

TO SERVE
1 recipe quantity Boiled Long-Grain Rice (*see page 214*)

1 Prepare a bowl of ice-cold water and bring a saucepan of water to a boil. Add the sugar snap peas to the boiling water and blanch 1 to 2 minutes. Drain, then put the sugar snaps into the iced water to stop the cooking process. Set aside.

2 Heat the oil in a skillet or saucepan over medium-high heat. Add the beef and cook, stirring occasionally, 3 minutes, or until sealed and beginning to brown. Add the onion and cook 2 to 3 minutes, until soft and translucent. Then add the carrots and cook 3 minutes, or until almost tender.

3 Tip in the potatoes, parsnip, daikon, dashi, sake and sugar. Bring to a boil and then push the ingredients around the pan, making sure the vegetables are covered by the dashi. Reduce the heat to low, cover and simmer 20 minutes. Add the shoyu and prepared sugar snap peas and cook, covered, 5 minutes longer. Serve immediately with boiled rice.

BIBIMBAP

'Bibim' in Korean means to mix and 'bap' means rice, so this dish literally translates as mixed rice. There is a popular variation of Bibimbap, known as Dol Sot Bibimbap, where the cooked rice is spread over the base of a stone pot and becomes crunchy during cooking. The other cooked ingredients are arranged on the rice and then a raw egg is added just before serving and stirred into the rice to cook it.

SERVES 4
PREPARATION TIME 30 minutes, plus 25 minutes freezing and soaking time
COOKING TIME 45 minutes

7-ounce beef fillet, wrapped and semifrozen 25 minutes (*see page 217*)
2 tablespoons sunflower oil
1 garlic clove, finely chopped
1 tablespoon light soy sauce
6 dried shiitake mushrooms, soaked, drained and cut into thin strips (*see page 217*)
1 teaspoon sesame oil
4½ ounces bean sprouts
1 small carrot, cut into matchsticks
1 zucchini, thinly sliced
7 ounces baby spinach leaves
4 eggs
1 recipe quantity Boiled Short-Grain Rice (*see page 214*)
freshly ground black pepper

TO SERVE
1 tablespoon sesame seeds
Korean hot pepper paste

1 Heat a skillet over medium-high heat, then add the sesame seeds and dry-fry a few minutes until the seeds begin to pop. Tip onto a plate and set aside.

2 Remove the partially frozen beef from the freezer and discard the plastic wrap. Using a sharp knife, cut the beef against the grain into ⅛-inch slices.

3 Heat 1 tablespoon of the sunflower oil in a skillet over medium-high heat. Add the garlic and stir-fry 1 minute, then add the beef and stir-fry 5 to 6 minutes until brown and cooked through. Add the soy sauce and season with pepper. Remove the beef from the pan and keep warm. Still over medium-high heat, add the shiitake mushrooms to the pan and stir-fry 2 minutes, then drizzle with the sesame oil. Remove the mushrooms from the pan, using a slotted spoon, set aside and keep warm. Repeat the process, without adding the sesame oil, with the bean sprouts and then the carrot.

4 Meanwhile, steam the zucchini 5 minutes, or until soft, and set aside. Steam the spinach 2 to 3 minutes until wilted, then drain, squeeze out any excess water and set aside.

5 Heat the remaining sunflower oil in a large skillet over medium heat and fry the eggs about 3 minutes each—the yolks should still be runny. Meanwhile, gently warm the beef and vegetables in a separate skillet.

6 To assemble, first divide the warm cooked rice into the serving bowls, and then the beef and vegetables. Put a fried egg in the center of each bowl. Sprinkle with the sesame seeds before serving with the Korean hot pepper paste on the side.

sesame barbecued beef

Bulgogi is one of two dishes (*see* Pak Choi Kimchi, *on page 36, for the other*) that really stuck with me after my first visit to Korea. The beef was very thinly sliced and gently marinated, then served raw on a platter with vegetables for each guest to cook on a shared grill at the table. Keeping the delicious, clean flavors, here is a modern take on the traditional dish with everything cooked in a skillet instead.

SERVES 4
PREPARATION TIME 15 minutes, plus 1 hour 25 minutes freezing and marinating time
COOKING TIME 20 minutes

1 pound 2 ounces rib-eye steak or sirloin, wrapped and semifrozen 25 minutes (*see page 217*)
3½ tablespoons light soy sauce
2 tablespoons sugar
2 tablespoons sesame oil
3 garlic cloves, finely chopped
½-inch piece of ginger-root, peeled and finely chopped
1 onion, sliced
2 tablespoons sesame seeds
1 tablespoon sunflower oil
2 scallions, finely chopped

TO SERVE
1 recipe quantity Boiled Long-Grain Rice (*see page 214*)

1 Remove the partially frozen beef from the freezer and discard the plastic wrap. Using a sharp knife, cut the beef against the grain into ⅛-inch slices, or even thinner if possible.

2 Put the beef in a large bowl with the soy sauce, sugar, sesame oil, garlic, ginger and onion, and mix well. Cover with plastic wrap and leave to marinate in the refrigerator about 1 hour.

3 Meanwhile, heat a skillet over medium-high heat, then add the sesame seeds and dry-fry a few minutes until the seeds begin to pop. Tip onto a plate and set aside.

4 Heat the sunflower oil in a cast-iron grill pan or heavy-bottomed skillet over high heat. When the oil begins to smoke, add the marinated beef and cook a few seconds before turning the heat down to medium-high. Spread out the meat in the pan, laying it as flat as possible so it cooks evenly. Cook 10 to 15 minutes, turning occasionally, until the beef is browned and tender.

5 One minute before the end of cooking, add the scallions. Sprinkle with the toasted sesame seeds and serve immediately with boiled rice.

sea bream nigirizushi

Nigirizushi is one of the most popular Japanese sushi. It is also called hand-formed sushi, because the rice is pressed and molded by hand into an oblong shape. I've used short-grain rice because it is readily available and gives a similar texture to sushi rice. It also takes less time to cook, which means these delicious morsels are quick to make. The blushing pink and thinly sliced pieces of sea bream taste great, though you could use other kinds of seafood.

SERVES 4
PREPARATION TIME 15 minutes, plus cooking the rice

7-ounce boneless, skinless sea bream or sea bass fillet
½ recipe quantity Boiled Short-Grain Rice, cooled (*see page 214*)
1 teaspoon wasabi

TO SERVE
wasabi
shoyu
Pickled Ginger (*see page 213*)

1 Place the fish fillet horizontally to you on a cutting board. Angle the knife at 45° to the fillet and cut the fillet against the grain into slices of about 1¼ inches wide and ⅛ to ¼-inch thick.

2 Moisten your hands with water, to avoid the rice sticking, and scoop up about 1 tablespoon of rice with one hand. Put it in the palm of your other hand and shape the rice into a 2- x 1-inch oblong with rounded corners. Take a slice of the prepared sea bream in one hand and smear over a small amount of wasabi. Place the rice on top of the slice of fish, then gently press down on the rice to stick them together. Turn the nigirizushi over and press the top and the sides to make sure the fish is firmly in place. Continue until all the remaining rice and fish are used up. Serve with wasabi, shoyu and pickled ginger.

korean-style makizushi

SERVES 4
PREPARATION TIME 45 minutes,
  plus 20 minutes cooling time
COOKING TIME 10 minutes, plus
  cooking the rice

4 teaspoons sesame seeds
1 recipe quantity Boiled
  Short-Grain Rice
  (*see page 214*)
2 tablespoons sesame oil
4 nori sheets (8 x 7 inches)

FILLING
2 eggs
1 teaspoon sunflower oil
7 ounces baby spinach leaves
½ carrot, cut into matchsticks
½ cucumber, halved
  lengthwise, seeded and
  cut into strips
12 seafood or shrimp sticks
fine sea salt

DIPPING SAUCE
2 tablespoons light soy sauce
1 tablespoon rice vinegar
1¼ tablespoons lemon juice

1 Heat a skillet over medium-high heat, then add the sesame seeds and dry-fry a few minutes until the seeds begin to pop. Tip half the sesame seeds into a mini food processor and grind to a fine powder. Set the other half of the sesame seeds aside.

2 To make the dipping sauce, whisk all the ingredients together with the ground sesame seeds until well combined. Set aside.

3 Transfer the cooked rice to a large wooden bowl or a nonmetallic baking dish. Add the sesame oil and remaining toasted sesame seeds and gently fold through the rice using a spatula. Level the rice, cover with a damp dish towel and set aside to cool to room temperature.

4 To make the filling, beat the eggs together with a pinch of salt in a small bowl. Pour the sunflower oil into a large, heavy-bottomed skillet over medium-high heat, then use a piece of paper towel to grease the pan evenly and soak up any excess oil. When the pan is hot, pour in the beaten eggs and turn the heat down to low. Cook the omelet 3 minutes on each side, until cooked through but not colored. Set aside to cool, then remove from the pan and cut into strips.

5 Meanwhile, bring a saucepan of salted water to a boil, add the spinach and cook about 30 seconds. Drain and refresh under cold running water. Squeeze out any excess liquid and pat dry with paper towels. Set aside.

6 Cover a bamboo sushi mat with plastic wrap and place on a clean surface with a long side closest to you. Leaving a gap of about ¾ inch at the edge nearest to you, place a nori sheet, rough-side up, on the mat. Moisten one of your hands to help stop the rice from sticking to it, then scoop up one-quarter of the rice and spread it evenly over two-thirds of the nori sheet, leaving a small gap at each end. Place 4 to 6 strips of omelet, a small handful of spinach, 2 to 3 strips of carrot, 2 to 3 strips of cucumber and 3 seafood sticks horizontally along the middle of the rice.

7 Bring up the bottom edge of the mat, fold it over the filling and then roll the nori up into a cylinder, pressing firmly at the same time to make sure the makizushi is tight and compact. Put a few grains of cooked rice along the end of the nori sheet and press firmly to seal. Give the mat a final press to create a tight roll. Set the roll aside and cover with plastic wrap. Repeat to make 3 more rolls.

8 To finish, lightly moisten the blade of a sharp knife and cut each roll into 5 or 6 rounds. Serve with the dipping sauce.

Tempura Shrimp Temaki

When I visit a Japanese restaurant, I always order Tempura and Temaki. Tempura is a dish of seafood or vegetables coated in a light batter, then deep-fried, and Temaki is a conelike sushi that is pretty to look at and tasty to eat. I've created Tempura Shrimp Temaki so that you can enjoy both of these delicious dishes in one!

MAKES 14
PREPARATION TIME 1 hour
35 minutes
COOKING TIME 1 hour, plus
cooking the rice

heaping ¾ cup all-purpose
flour, plus extra for dusting
2 tablespoons cornstarch
1 teaspoon baking powder
1 egg yolk
3 tablespoons sesame seeds
2 cups sunflower oil, for
deep-frying
14 raw, peeled jumbo shrimp,
heads removed, with tails left
on and deveined
(*see page 216*)
3 tablespoons light
mayonnaise
2 tablespoons lemon juice
1 scallion, green part only,
finely chopped
7 nori sheets (8 x 7 inches),
halved lengthwise
1 recipe quantity Boiled
Short-Grain Rice, cooled
(*see page 214*)
1 small cucumber, quartered,
seeded and cut into strips
1 small carrot, cut into
matchsticks
sea salt

TO SERVE
shoyu
wasabi paste (optional)

1 Mix together the flour, cornstarch and baking powder in a mixing bowl. In a separate bowl, lightly whisk together the egg yolk and add ⅔ cup ice-cold sparkling natural mineral water. Pour the egg mixture into the dry ingredients and lightly fold it through using a whisk. Don't overmix the batter—it should stay lumpy. Put the batter bowl into a larger bowl that is half filled with ice cubes to keep the batter cold at all times.

2 Heat a skillet over medium-high heat, then add the sesame seeds and dry-fry a few minutes until the seeds begin to pop. Tip onto a plate and set aside.

3 Heat the oil in a deep, heavy-bottomed saucepan to 325°F, or until a small piece of bread dropped into the hot oil turns brown in 20 seconds. Lightly coat each shrimp in a little flour mixture, shaking off the excess. Dip the shrimp into the batter, then gently slide it into the oil. Fry 2 to 3 shrimp at a time, 2 to 3 minutes until a light golden brown. Remove the shrimp, using a slotted spoon, and drain on paper towels. Repeat until all the shrimp have been cooked.

4 Combine the mayonnaise, lemon juice, scallion and a pinch of salt in a small bowl. To assemble, place a nori sheet on a clean surface with the longest edge closest to you, rough-side up. Moisten one of your hands with water, then scoop up about 2 heaping tablespoons of the rice. Spread the rice evenly over the half of the nori sheet closest to you, leaving the bottom corner free of rice.

5 Spread 1 to 2 teaspoons of the mayonnaise mixture evenly over the rice and sprinkle with the toasted sesame seeds. Add 1 tempura shrimp, 2 to 3 cucumber strips and 2 to 3 carrot strips diagonally on top of the rice. Fold the bottom corner of the nori over the ingredients to form a pointed end and then continue to roll to make a cone shape. Stick one or two rice grains at the corner end and press firmly to seal. Continue until all the ingredients are used. Serve with shoyu, mixed with a little wasabi paste, if liked, for dipping.

soy & mirin tuna on soba noodles

"Soba" is the word for buckwheat in Japanese and there are two types of soba noodles—the normal dark brown noodle with the natural color of buckwheat and the green-colored "green tea" soba. You can use either, but the green tea version looks very pretty and gives a fresher, lighter taste to the dish.

SERVES 4
PREPARATION TIME 15 minutes, plus 35 minutes cooling and marinating time
COOKING TIME 15 minutes, plus cooking the noodles

14-ounce skinless tuna loin
½ cup shoyu
scant ½ cup mirin
1 tablespoon sugar
½-inch piece of ginger root, peeled and finely grated, pulp discarded, juice reserved
1 tablespoon sesame seeds
12 ounces cooked green tea soba or buckwheat soba noodles (*see page 215*)
1 teaspoon sunflower oil
1 scallion, finely chopped, to serve

1 Bring a saucepan of water to a boil, then poach the tuna loin 25 to 30 seconds to seal. Remove the tuna from the water, pat dry and transfer to a plate to cool about 5 minutes.

2 Meanwhile, mix the shoyu, mirin, sugar and ginger juice in a large bowl. Add the seared tuna and thoroughly coat with the marinade. Cover with plastic wrap and leave to marinate in the refrigerator 30 minutes.

3 Heat a skillet over medium-high heat, then add the sesame seeds and dry-fry a few minutes until the seeds begin to pop. Tip onto a plate and set aside.

4 Remove the tuna from the marinade and strain the marinade into a small saucepan. Simmer the marinade over medium heat for 2 to 3 minutes until slightly thickened. Remove from the heat and keep warm.

5 Heat the oil in a large skillet over high heat, then add the tuna and sear 1 to 2 minutes on each side. The outer layer should be cooked and golden brown but the inside should remain raw—don't cook the tuna completely through. Transfer the tuna to a cutting board, angle a sharp knife at 45° to the surface and slice against the grain into ¼-inch strips.

6 Meanwhile, while the tuna is searing, bring another saucepan of water to a boil and plunge in the soba noodles a few seconds to heat through. Drain and divide the noodles into deep soup bowls, then top with the tuna. Drizzle the tuna with the reduced marinade. Sprinkle with the toasted sesame seeds and chopped scallion before serving hot or cold.

korean spicy seafood noodle soup

SERVES 4 to 6
PREPARATION TIME 45 minutes
   to 1 hour, plus making the stock
COOKING TIME 30 minutes, plus
   cooking the noodles

1 tablespoon sesame seeds
½ of a 1-ounce package of
   dried wakame
1 pound 2 ounces mussels,
   scrubbed, beards removed
1 tablespoon sunflower oil
1 onion, sliced
3 garlic cloves, finely chopped
½-inch piece of ginger-root,
   peeled and finely chopped
4 dried shiitake mushrooms,
   soaked, drained and cut into
   thin strips (*see page 217*)
1 tablespoon Korean red
   pepper powder or cayenne
   pepper
1 recipe quantity Chicken
   Stock (*see page 210*)
¼ Chinese cabbage, cored
   and cut into bite-size pieces
1 tablespoon light soy sauce
1 tablespoon Chili Oil
   (*see page 211*)
10½ ounces raw, peeled jumbo
   shrimp, tails left on, deveined
   (*see page 216*)
14 ounces squid, scored with a
   crisscross pattern and cut
   into bite-size pieces
   (*see page 216*)
1 pound 2 ounces cooked fresh
   fine egg noodles or 12 ounces
   dried fine egg noodles
   (*see page 215*)
2 scallions, finely chopped

1 Heat a skillet over medium-high heat, then add the sesame seeds and dry-fry a few minutes until the seeds begin to pop. Tip onto a plate and set aside.

2 Soak the dried wakame in a small bowl in warm water about 10 minutes, until it rehydrates. Drain, rinse and set aside.

3 Tap any mussels that are only partly opened on a hard surface and discard those that don't shut. Put the mussels in a saucepan over high heat and steam 3 to 4 minutes, until the shells open. There is no need to add any additional liquid to the pan because the mussels will steam in the liquid they release themselves. However, be sure to discard any that don't open fully after steaming. Once cooked, remove and discard the mussel shells. Set the mussels aside.

4 Heat the sunflower oil in a large saucepan over medium-high heat. Add the onion and cook 2 to 3 minutes until soft and translucent, then add the garlic and ginger and cook 2 minutes, or until fragrant. Add the shiitake mushrooms and Korean red pepper powder or cayenne pepper and cook, stirring continuously, 1 minute. Remove from the heat and add the chicken stock.

5 Return the pan to the heat and bring the chicken stock to a boil. Add the Chinese cabbage and cook 3 to 4 minutes until tender. Add the soy sauce and chili oil, and then add the shrimp and squid. Bring to a boil a few seconds, then reduce the heat to low, cover and simmer 5 to 6 minutes until the shrimp turn pink and are cooked through and the squid is tender. Three minutes before the end of cooking, add the mussels to heat them through.

6 Divide the hot, cooked noodles into deep soup bowls, then spoon the shrimp, squid, cabbage and mussels into the bowls.

7 Bring the chicken stock to a vigorous boil. Add the scallions and prepared wakame to the bowls, then ladle in the piping hot stock. Sprinkle with the toasted sesame seeds and serve immediately.

japanese pork dumplings

Growing up in a Chinese family meant that we often made and ate dumplings. I remember lovely times in the kitchen helping my mom make the gyoza wrappers from scratch and preparing the ingredients. As time has passed, my style of cooking dumplings has evolved, and I have started using different ingredients, such as watercress, which makes this dish explode with flavor, instead of the usual cabbage.

MAKES 28
PREPARATION TIME about 1 hour, plus 1 hour marinating and resting time
COOKING TIME 10 to 20 minutes

6 ounces white cabbage, halved and core removed
2¾ ounces watercress, chopped
5 scallions, finely chopped
9½ ounces ground pork
7 garlic cloves, finely chopped
¾-inch piece of ginger-root, peeled and finely chopped
1 tablespoon cornstarch
1 tablespoon sesame oil
3 tablespoons shoyu
1 tablespoon sake
1 teaspoon mirin
1 teaspoon sugar
1 or 2 tablespoons sunflower oil
freshly ground black pepper

GYOZA WRAPPERS
1¾ cups all-purpose flour, plus extra for dusting
sunflower oil, for oiling
sea salt

TO SERVE
shoyu
Chili Oil (*see page 211—optional*)

1 Bring a large saucepan of water to a boil, add the cabbage leaves and blanch for 1 minute. Remove the leaves with long-handled tongs and plunge immediately into a bowl of ice-cold water to stop the cooking process. Drain, pat dry with a dish towel, squeezing out as much water as possible, and then finely chop. Transfer to a large bowl and add the watercress and scallions.

2 Mix together the pork, garlic, ginger, cornstarch, sesame oil, shoyu, sake, mirin and sugar in a large bowl until well combined, then season with pepper. Add the cabbage and watercress mixture, and stir to combine. Cover with plastic wrap and leave to marinate in the refrigerator 1 hour.

3 Meanwhile, to make the gyoza wrappers, put the flour and a pinch of salt in a large mixing bowl and make a well in the center. Slowly pour in generous ⅓ cup cold water and combine with the flour to form a soft dough. Turn the dough out onto a lightly floured surface and knead 10 minutes, until it is smooth and elastic. Shape the dough into a ball, transfer to a lightly oiled bowl, cover with a damp dish towel and let rest 1 hour.

4 Turn the dough out again onto a lightly floured surface, roll it into a cylinder and divide into 4 to 5 equal portions. Take a portion of the dough and roll flat until it is about 1/16 to ⅛ inch thick, then, using a 3½-inch cookie cutter, cut out neat circles. Dust the surface of the wrappers lightly with flour so they don't stick together, then stack them on a lightly floured plate. Repeat with the remaining dough portions. Keep any dough you are not using covered with a damp dish towel to prevent it from drying out.

5 Place a small bowl of water nearby to use for sealing the dumplings. Set a gyoza wrapper on the forefront of your hand, then put a heaped tablespoon of the pork filling in the center. Shape the filling into an oblong shape and flatten it slightly. Moisten around the edge of the wrapper with water and bring one side of the wrapper over the filling to form a half-moon shape.

6 Press one corner of the wrapper together to seal, then pinch the edge of the top half of the wrapper next to the seal into a pleat, pushing the pleat into the edge of the bottom half of the wrapper to seal. Continue to work around the edge to the other corner. There should be 6 to 8 pleats and the bottom half of the wrapper should remain flat.

7 When you've finished pleating the pastry, press gently into the back of the pastry to form a crescent shape. Transfer the gyoza to a lightly floured plate and cover with a damp dish towel while you make the remaining dumplings.

8 Heat the sunflower oil in a large skillet over medium-high heat, then arrange the gyoza in the pan. Leave a bit of space between each dumpling to stop the gyoza from sticking together. Cook 3 to 4 minutes, then pour in enough hot water to half cover the gyoza. Cover, reduce the heat to medium and cook until the liquid has evaporated.

9 Remove the lid and cook 4 to 5 minutes longer until the bottom of the gyoza becomes brown and crisp. Depending on the size of the skillet, you may need to cook the gyoza in batches. Serve immediately with shoyu and chili oil, if liked.

BOK CHOY KIMCHI

Kimchi is one of the best-known side dishes in Korean cuisine, and is served at almost every meal. There are many varieties of kimchi, and how they are made varies from region to region and by season. Varieties from the north tend to be a little less spicy than those from the south, where a lot more Korean red pepper powder is used. Whereas cabbage kimchi is the most common, other vegetables, such as bok choy and cucumber, are also often used.

MAKES about 1½ pounds
PREPARATION TIME 30 minutes, plus 4 to 5 hours resting time and 2 days pickling

2 pounds 4 ounces bok choy, roughly chopped into pieces 1¼ inches wide
½ cup sea salt
1¼-inch piece of ginger-root, peeled and roughly chopped
6 garlic cloves, roughly chopped
1 onion, roughly chopped
½ red apple, peeled and roughly chopped
2 tablespoons Korean red pepper powder or cayenne pepper
2 tablespoons sugar
4 scallions, chopped

1 Put the bok choy in a colander and rinse under cold running water, drain well and transfer to a large bowl or saucepan. Mix the salt together with 2 cups water until dissolved, then pour the briny liquid over the bok choy. Using both your hands, mix the bok choy and water together, making sure it is well coated with the brine. Let stand 4 to 5 hours at room temperature.

2 Rinse the bok choy 2 to 3 times under cold running water to remove the brine, then squeeze out the excess liquid and put in a large bowl. Put the ginger, garlic, onion and apple in a food processor or blender and blend until smooth. Transfer the paste to a small bowl and mix in the Korean red pepper powder and sugar. Pour the mixture over the bok choy and tip in the scallions.

3 Wearing rubber gloves, thoroughly mix everything together using your hands, then transfer the seasoned bok choy to a large sterilized preserving jar and seal with a tight-fitting lid. Let the kimchi ferment 24 to 48 hours in a cool, dark place before putting in the refrigerator, where it will keep up to 1 month. Serve cold.

green tea & sesame seed ice cream

Green tea is a wonderfully versatile ingredient that, apart from making a refreshing hot drink, is an excellent food coloring for savory dishes, cakes and desserts. Bright green ice cream is always a welcome sight on a hot summer's day, but with the subtle earthy flavor that comes from the inclusion of toasted ground black sesame, this ice cream is delicious eaten any time of the year.

SERVES 4
PREPARATION TIME 15 minutes, plus minimum 5 to 6 hours cooling and freezing time
COOKING TIME 15 minutes

2 tablespoons black sesame
  seeds
2 cups low-fat milk
scant ½ cup heavy cream
2 egg yolks
heaping ½ cup sugar
2 teaspoons green tea powder

1 Heat a skillet over medium-high heat, then add the sesame seeds and dry-fry a few minutes until the seeds begin to pop. Remove from the pan and put in a mini food processor, or use a mortar and pestle and grind to a coarse powder.

2 Pour the milk and heavy cream into a saucepan, place over medium heat and bring just to a boil. Remove from the heat.

3 Meanwhile, using an electric mixer or whisk, beat the egg yolks, sugar and green tea powder until light and creamy. With the motor still running, slowly pour in the milk mixture until light and fluffy.

4 Pour the mixture into a clean saucepan over low heat and cook, stirring continuously, 10 minutes, or until it forms a thick custard. Be careful not to overheat or the custard may curdle. Remove from the heat and pour through a fine strainer into a clean bowl. Stir in the ground black sesame seed powder.

5 Let the custard cool completely and then pour it into an ice-cream machine. Churn until thick and frozen, according to the manufacturer's instructions, and then transfer to a plastic or metal container, cover and freeze up to 2 weeks.

CHINA

Chinese cuisine is made up of dishes from the many different regions in China, each varying in taste and appearance. But what is common to all the wonderful dishes that make up Chinese cuisine is the balance of flavors, textures and colors. These factors are considered to be as important as eating a meal that has a balance of "Yin" and "Yang" ingredients. "Yin" foods, such as Chinese Roast Duck Pancake Rolls (*see pages 42 to 43*) and the soupy dish, Chinese BBQ Pork Noodle Soup (*see page 45*), are thought to have a cooling effect on the body, while "Yang" foods, such as Beef & Asparagus Stir-Fry (*see page 52*) and Chicken & Sticky Rice in Lotus Leaves (*see page 57*) are considered to have warming properties. Rice is one of the staple foods of Chinese cooking. It is always steamed and is served at every meal. Noodles are almost as indispensable as rice, and are normally stir-fried or served in a hot broth.

Key ingredients vary from region to region, but one thing that is used frequently, everywhere, is fresh ginger, a pungent and spicy root. It lifts the flavor of simple dishes, such as Cantonese Steamed Fish (*see page 54*) and gives depth to other dishes such as Sichuan Mapo Tofu (*see page 48*). Soy sauce is possibly the most important ingredient in Chinese cooking, followed closely by Chinese rice wine. Sesame, Rice Wine & Soy Chicken (*see page 40*) is one very tasty example of a dish that makes good use of both.

sesame, rice wine & soy chicken

This dish originates from the Jiangxi province in southern China, but has become a popular, classic Taiwanese dish. Traditionally, this dish calls for a cup each of sesame oil, rice wine and soy sauce and is simmered with a chicken in a claypot over high heat until all the sauce has been absorbed. However, I've used a lot less to make it less oily and salty.

SERVES 4
PREPARATION TIME 15 minutes
COOKING TIME 25 to 30 minutes

1 pound 5 ounces boneless, skinless chicken thighs, cut into bite-size pieces
1 teaspoon sunflower oil
½-inch piece of ginger-root, peeled and cut into fine matchsticks
4 garlic cloves, whole and slightly crushed
2 scallions, cut into 2-inch pieces lengthwise
2 dried chilies, seeded and roughly chopped
½ cup Shaoxing rice wine
3 tablespoons light soy sauce
2 tablespoons sugar
2 tablespoons sesame oil
1 handful of basil leaves
1 handful of cilantro leaves

TO SERVE
1 recipe quantity Boiled Long-Grain Rice (*see page 214*)

1 Bring a saucepan of water to a boil and poach the chicken pieces for about 1 minute to seal. Drain and set aside.

2 Heat the sunflower oil in a skillet over high heat until the oil shimmers and starts to smoke. Add the ginger and stir-fry 1 minute, then add the garlic and stir-fry 1 minute longer. Stir in the scallions and dried chilies, and stir-fry 1 minute. Tip in the chicken, rice wine, soy sauce and sugar, cover the pan and cook 20 to 25 minutes until the liquid has evaporated and the chicken is cooked through, stirring occasionally.

3 Meanwhile, heat a flameproof claypot or a small Dutch oven over high heat until very hot. Transfer the chicken pieces from the pan into the claypot, add the sesame oil, basil and cilantro, and then cover with the lid. Let the chicken sizzle a few seconds, then serve immediately with boiled rice.

CHINESE ROAST DUCK PANCAKE ROLLS

This is an all-time favorite of mine and it never disappoints me—tender duck coated with a flavorsome, glistening glaze of soy sauce and light corn syrup, served in steamed pancakes. The most important part of the cooking process is resting the duck in an airy place to dehydrate the skin. This drying process results in a delicate, crispy skin when the duck is cooked.

SERVES 4 to 6
PREPARATION TIME 25 minutes, plus 3 to 7 hours marinating and resting time
COOKING TIME about 1 hour

4-pound duck
1 tablespoon sea salt
½ teaspoon Ground Toasted Sichuan Pepper (*see page 212*)
2 tablespoons sugar
1 tablespoon Shaoxing rice wine
2 star anise
2-inch cinnamon stick
3 scallions, halved
1¼-inch piece of ginger-root, peeled and sliced

PANCAKES
2 cups all-purpose flour, plus extra for dusting
¼ teaspoon sea salt
1 tablespoon sesame oil
sunflower oil, for oiling

GLAZE
1 tablespoon light corn syrup or honey
1 tablespoon sugar
1 tablespoon light soy sauce

1 Rinse the duck thoroughly inside and out under cold running water and pat dry inside and out with paper towels. Lightly prick the skin all over with a fork. Rub the salt, Sichuan pepper, sugar and rice wine onto the skin and put the star anise, cinnamon stick, scallions and ginger in the cavity. Secure the cavity closed with a metal skewer, then transfer the duck to a platter, cover with plastic wrap and leave to marinate in the refrigerator about 30 minutes.

2 Bring a large saucepan of water to a boil, then slowly lower in the duck so it is completely submerged. Boil 5 minutes. Remove the pan from the heat and drain the duck in a colander. Discard the ingredients in the cavity, sit the duck on a wire rack and leave in a well-ventilated area 5 to 6 hours until all the moisture has evaporated. Alternatively, put in the refrigerator 2 to 3 hours.

3 Meanwhile, to prepare the pancakes, mix the flour and salt together in a large bowl. Gradually pour in ¾ cup hot water and mix with a wooden spoon until it forms a soft, smooth dough. Add a few extra splashes of cold water if the dough is dry. Turn the dough out onto a lightly floured surface and knead 10 to 15 minutes until very smooth, then put in a lightly oiled bowl and cover with a damp dish towel or plastic wrap. Set aside 30 minutes.

4 Pour the sesame oil into a shallow dish. Turn the dough out onto a lightly floured surface, roll it into a cylinder and divide into 8 to 10 portions of about 1 ounce each. Take a piece of dough and shape into a ball. Dip the dough in the sesame oil, turning until coated all around, then place the ball on a clean surface and press into a flat disk. Using a rolling pin, roll into a 7-inch disk about ¹⁄₁₆ inch thick. Place the disk on a lightly floured surface and repeat with the remaining dough portions.

1 tablespoon rice wine vinegar
¼ teaspoon five-spice powder

TO SERVE
6 scallions, cut into fine
   matchsticks
½ cucumber, halved
   lengthwise, seeded and
   cut into strips
hoisin sauce or plum sauce

5 Heat the oven to 400°F. To prepare the glaze, mix all the ingredients in a small bowl. Line a roasting pan with a sheet of foil, place a wire rack on top and set the duck on the rack. Using a pastry brush, brush the glaze mixture all over the duck.

6 Turn the duck so the breast is facing down. Position the roasting pan on the second-lowest shelf in the oven and cook the duck for 15 minutes. After 15 minutes, turn the duck breast-side up. Lower the temperature to 350°F and continue to cook the duck 1 hour longer, or until cooked. After about 45 minutes, brush the glaze mixture all over the duck again. When the duck is cooked, the juices should run clear when the tip of a sharp knife is inserted into the thickest part of the meat. Remove the duck from the oven, pour out any fat or juices from the cavity and set it aside.

7 Meanwhile, heat a skillet over high heat until hot, then reduce the heat to low and cook a pancake 1 to 2 minutes on each side until it blisters and light brown spots start to form. Set aside, cover with a damp dish towel and cook the remaining pancakes.

8 Just before the duck is ready, steam the pancakes in a bamboo or electric steamer 5 to 7 minutes until cooked through.

9 Carve the duck meat into slices, removing the skin if it is too fatty, and put on a serving plate with the scallions, cucumber and hoisin sauce for the pancake rolls to be assembled at the table.

CHINESE BBQ PORK NOODLE SOUP

BBQ pork, known in China as Char Siu, is one of the most popular Guangdong dishes and goes well with both rice and noodles. It can also be used as the filling for Chicken & Vegetable Steamed Buns (*see pages 58–59*). For a really tasty dish, marinate the pork well in advance so that the flavors penetrate the meat.

SERVES 4 to 6
PREPARATION TIME 25 minutes, plus minimum 6 hours marinating time and making the stock
COOKING TIME 50 minutes, plus cooking the noodles

1 pound 12 ounces piece of boneless pork loin roast, excess fat removed
4 tablespoons light soy sauce
1 tablespoon oyster sauce
2 tablespoons sugar
3 tablespoons light corn syrup or honey
1 tablespoon Shaoxing rice wine
1¼-inch piece of ginger-root, peeled, lightly crushed and sliced
7 ounces broccoli rabe, trimmed
1 pound 5 ounces cooked fresh fine egg noodles or 12 ounces dried fine egg noodles (*see page 215*)
1 recipe quantity Chicken Stock (*see page 210*)
2 scallions, sliced
freshly ground black pepper

1 Put the pork in a deep dish or bowl. In a separate bowl, mix together the light soy sauce, oyster sauce, sugar, 2 tablespoons of the light corn syrup, rice wine and ginger. Season with pepper, then pour the mixture over the pork and then, using your hands, rub the marinade into the pork until it is well coated. Cover with plastic wrap and leave to marinate in the refrigerator 6 hours or, for an even better flavor, overnight.

2 Heat the oven to 350°F. Remove the pork from the refrigerator and strain off the marinade, keeping the liquid and discarding the solids. Stir the remaining light corn syrup into the marinade. Line a roasting pan with foil, place a wire rack on top and set the pork onto the rack. Place the pan on the second-lowest shelf in the oven and roast the pork 25 minutes. Using long-handled tongs, turn over the pork and cook 25 minutes longer, or until cooked through. When the pork is cooked, the juices should run clear when the tip of a sharp knife is inserted into the thickest part of the meat. Five minutes before the end of cooking, generously brush the marinade all over the pork. Remove from the oven and keep warm.

3 Bring a saucepan of water to a boil and blanch the broccoli rabe 2 to 3 minutes until tender. Meanwhile, divide the warm, cooked noodles into deep serving bowls. Divide the blanched broccoli into the bowls of noodles.

4 Pour the chicken stock into a saucepan and bring to a gentle boil over medium heat. Meanwhile, transfer the pork to a cutting board and cut against the grain into ¼-inch slices. Divide the pork into the soup bowls and sprinkle with the scallions. Ladle the piping hot stock onto the noodles and serve immediately.

Dan Dan Noodles

Egg noodles topped with ground pork, drizzled with a vinegary sauce and giving off a hint of spice from chili oil make this famous dish from Chengdu. Vendors used to transport their noodles in baskets hanging from a bamboo pole, called a dan in Chinese, giving this dish the name Dan Dan Noodles.

SERVES 4 to 6
PREPARATION TIME 15 minutes, plus 25 minutes soaking time
COOKING TIME 20 to 25 minutes, plus cooking the noodles

2 tablespoons sunflower oil
1 garlic clove, peeled and finely chopped
½-inch piece of ginger root, peeled and finely chopped
1-ounce package dried mushrooms, such as shiitake, porcini or Chinese mushrooms, soaked, drained and roughly chopped (*see page 217*)
12 ounces ground pork
2 teaspoons light soy sauce
1 tablespoon sesame oil
1 tablespoon Shaoxing rice wine
1 tablespoon finely diced carrot
1 tablespoon finely sliced green beans
1 pound 5 ounces cooked fresh fine egg noodles or 12 ounces dried fine egg noodles (*see page 215*)
freshly ground black pepper
2 scallions, minced, to serve

SAUCE
5 tablespoons light soy sauce
2 tablespoons dark soy sauce
2 tablespoons balsamic vinegar

TO SERVE
Chili Oil (*see page 211— optional*)

1 To make the sauce, mix together the light and dark soy sauces and vinegar with 4 tablespoons warm water in a small bowl. Set aside.

2 Heat 1 tablespoon of the sunflower oil in a skillet over medium-high heat. Add the garlic and ginger, and fry until they start to turn light golden brown, then add the mushrooms and cook 1 minute.

3 Add the ground pork, breaking up the lumps. Cook, stirring occasionally, 5 to 10 minutes until browned and cooked through, then stir in the soy sauce and sesame oil, and season with pepper. Add the rice wine and 3 tablespoons water, and simmer 3 minutes longer. Set aside and keep warm.

4 Meanwhile, heat the remaining 1 tablespoon of oil in a skillet over medium heat and stir-fry the carrot and green beans 1 to 2 minutes.

5 Divide the cooked noodles into deep soup bowls, then drizzle with the sauce mixture. Add the pork mixture, carrots and green beans to the bowls, then sprinkle with the scallions. For a bit of spiciness, add 2 or 3 teaspoons of the chili oil, including the chili flakes, if liked. Serve immediately.

sweet & spicy pork belly

This is a popular dish, regularly cooked in many Chinese households. The method of cooking, however, varies by region. In southern China, the use of dark soy sauce is favored because it enhances the color of the dish, whereas in northern China, sugar, which gives a glossy and caramelized look, is used instead. A good-quality piece of pork belly is essential for getting the melt-in-your-mouth result that comes from braising the meat in the aromatic sauce.

SERVES 4 to 6
PREPARATION TIME 15 minutes
COOKING TIME about 1 hour

1 pound 12 ounces bite-size pieces of pork belly
1 tablespoon sunflower oil
1 star anise
2-inch cinnamon stick
2 dried chilies, seeded and roughly chopped
3 garlic cloves, finely chopped
¼ teaspoon Sichuan peppercorns
2 tablespoons honey
2 tablespoons light soy sauce
1 tablespoon dark soy sauce
1 tablespoon Shaoxing rice wine
2 scallions, cut into pieces 2½ inches long
¾-inch piece of ginger root, peeled and sliced

TO SERVE
1 recipe quantity Boiled Long-Grain Rice (*see page 214*)

1 Bring a saucepan of water to a boil, then lower in the pork belly and poach 3 minutes to seal. Drain and set aside.

2 Heat the oil in a saucepan over medium-high heat. Add the star anise, cinnamon stick and dried chilies, and stir-fry 2 to 3 minutes until fragrant. Add the garlic and stir-fry 1 to 2 minutes, then add the Sichuan peppercorns and stir-fry 1 minute, or until fragrant.

3 Add the poached pork belly and mix well, then add the honey, light and dark soy sauces, rice wine, scallions and ginger. Cook 5 minutes, stirring occasionally, then add scant ⅔ cup water. Bring to a boil and cook a few seconds.

4 Reduce the heat to low and simmer, covered, 45 minutes, or until the liquid has reduced and thickened and the pork is tender. Serve hot with boiled rice.

sichuan mapo tofu

This is a famous Sichuan dish that comes with a story. It is said that during the Qing Dynasty, a restaurant on the outskirts of Chengdu was well known for a delicious, very spicy tofu dish, which was made by the restaurateur's wife. She had pockmarks on her face, and as a result was called Mapo (ma means pockmark and po means elderly woman), so her signature dish was called Mapo Dou Fu.

SERVES 4
PREPARATION TIME 10 minutes
COOKING TIME 20 minutes

10½ ounces soft silken tofu,
  cut into bite-size cubes
1 tablespoon sunflower oil
½-inch piece of ginger-root,
  peeled and finely chopped
3 garlic cloves, finely chopped
7 ounces ground beef or pork
2 tablespoons chili bean paste
1 tablespoon light soy sauce
1 teaspoon sugar
1 teaspoon Ground Toasted
  Sichuan Pepper (*see page
  212*)
1 teaspoon cornstarch
2 scallions, roughly chopped,
  to serve

TO SERVE
14 ounces cooked egg noodles
  (*see page 215*)

1 Bring a large saucepan of water to a boil, then remove from the heat. Carefully tip the tofu into the water and set aside.

2 Heat the oil in a wok or skillet over medium-high heat. Add the ginger and garlic, and stir-fry 1 to 2 minutes until fragrant but not colored. Add the ground beef or pork, break up the lumps and cook, stirring occasionally, 5 minutes, or until starting to brown. Add the chili bean paste, soy sauce, sugar, ground Sichuan pepper and scant 1 cup water. Stir to combine and slowly bring to a boil.

3 Carefully drain the tofu and add it to the wok. Gently push the ingredients around the wok until the tofu pieces are coated with the sauce. Do not stir because it may break up the delicate tofu. Let it simmer 3 to 5 minutes until heated through.

4 Meanwhile, combine the cornstarch with 1 tablespoon water in a small bowl. Slowly pour the cornstarch mixture into the wok or pan and gently fold through. Sprinkle with the scallions and serve immediately with noodles.

sizzling beef with ginger & scallions

When I was little, as a Friday evening treat, my parents would often take my sister, brother and me out for dinner. There was a particular restaurant we loved that served lip-smacking frog legs on a cast-iron sizzle pan. That mouthwatering dish is the inspiration behind this sizzling beef dish.

SERVES 4
PREPARATION TIME 10 minutes, plus 40 minutes freezing and marinating time
COOKING TIME 15 minutes

1 pound 2 ounces sirloin steak, wrapped and semifrozen 25 minutes
(*see page 217*)
2 teaspoons cornstarch
2 tablespoons sunflower oil
¾-inch piece of ginger-root, peeled and cut into thin matchsticks
2 garlic cloves, finely chopped
2 tablespoons Shaoxing rice wine
2 tablespoons oyster sauce
3 scallions, cut lengthwise into pieces 2½ inches long
freshly ground black pepper

TO SERVE
1 recipe quantity Boiled Long-Grain Rice (*see page 214)*

1 Remove the partially frozen beef from the freezer and discard the plastic wrap. Using a sharp knife, cut the beef against the grain into ¼-inch slices. Put the beef in a large bowl with the cornstarch and toss together until the beef is well coated. Set aside 15 minutes.

2 Heat 1 tablespoon of the oil in a wok or large skillet over high heat until smoking hot. Tip in half the marinated beef and stir-fry 1 minute, or until sealed all around. Remove the beef from the pan, using a slotted spoon, and drain on paper towels. Make sure the wok is still smoking hot, then repeat with the remaining beef.

3 Heat the remaining tablespoon of oil in a clean wok or large skillet over medium-high heat. Add the ginger and garlic, and stir-fry 1 to 2 minutes until fragrant but not colored. Add the cooked beef slices and toss the ingredients a few seconds so everything is combined, then add the rice wine, oyster sauce and season with pepper. Cook 1 to 2 minutes, tossing occasionally to ensure the ingredients are well combined.

4 Meanwhile, heat a cast-iron grill pan, or heavy-bottomed skillet, either on the stovetop or by placing it in a very hot oven for about 5 minutes, and follow until it is smoking hot. Add the scallions and cook, turning occasionally, 1 to 2 minutes until golden brown all over.

5 Pour ¼ cup water into the wok or pan with the beef. Toss the ingredients so everything is well combined, then bring to a gentle boil a few seconds and toss again. Transfer the beef stir-fry to the grill pan and let sizzle a few seconds. Serve immediately with boiled rice.

beef & asparagus stir-fry

The wok is an essential piece of equipment in every Chinese kitchen. Its curved shape means it is hottest at the bottom and enables the heat to rise evenly up the sides. To give your stir-fries some "wok hei," which simply means the flavor and aroma imparted by the wok, the wok should be intensely hot before you add the ingredients.

SERVES 4 to 6
PREPARATION TIME 15 minutes, plus 55 minutes freezing and marinating time
COOKING TIME 10 minutes

1 pound 2 ounce piece beef fillet, wrapped and semifrozen 25 minutes (*see page 217*)
3 teaspoons cornstarch
3 tablespoons light soy sauce
1 tablespoon dark soy sauce
1 tablespoon oyster sauce
1 tablespoon sesame oil
2 tablespoons Shaoxing rice wine
1 teaspoon honey
3 tablespoons sunflower oil
7 ounces asparagus, cut into bite-size pieces
¼ teaspoon freshly ground black pepper
½-inch piece of ginger root, peeled and finely chopped
2 garlic cloves, finely chopped
sea salt

TO SERVE
1 recipe quantity Boiled Long-Grain Rice (*see page 214)*

1 Remove the partially frozen beef from the freezer and discard the plastic wrap. Using a sharp knife, cut the beef against the grain into ¼-inch slices.

2 Put the beef in a large bowl with 2 tablespoons of the cornstarch, 1 tablespoon of the light soy sauce, the dark soy sauce, oyster sauce, sesame oil, rice wine and honey, and toss until the beef is well coated in the marinade. Cover with plastic wrap and leave to marinate in the refrigerator 30 minutes.

3 Heat 1 tablespoon of the sunflower oil in a wok over high heat until smoking hot. Tip in half the marinated beef and stir-fry for 1 minute, or until sealed all around. Remove the beef from the wok, using a slotted spoon, and drain on paper towels. Make sure the wok is still smoking hot, then repeat with the remaining beef.

4 Meanwhile, prepare a large bowl of ice-cold water. Bring a saucepan of water to a boil, add a pinch of salt, tip in the asparagus and cook 2 minutes, or until al dente. Drain the asparagus and plunge it into the iced water to stop the cooking process.

5 Mix the remaining 2 tablespoons light soy sauce and pepper with 2 tablespoons water in a small bowl. In another bowl, mix together the remaining teaspoon of the cornstarch and 1 tablespoon of the sunflower oil, then slowly pour into the soy sauce mixture, stirring continuously.

6 Heat the remaining tablespoon of oil in a clean wok or large skillet over medium-high heat. Add the ginger and garlic, and stir-fry 1 to 2 minutes until fragrant but not colored. Drain the asparagus and add to the wok and stir-fry 1 minute. Add the beef and stir-fry 2 minutes, then add the cornstarch mixture. Toss the ingredients so everything is well combined, then bring to a gentle boil a few seconds. Serve immediately with boiled rice.

Lamb, Zucchini & Orange Stir-Fry

With the addition of pieces of orange and orange juice, this dish is fresh-tasting with a touch of citrus sweetness. Traditionally, lamb stir-fries are served with broccoli or asparagus, but here I give it a modern slant, using zucchini instead. The secret to making a delicious stir-fry in minutes is to slice the lamb thinly. It takes less time to cook and the succulent texture is preserved.

SERVES 4 to 6
PREPARATION TIME 15 minutes, plus 25 minutes freezing time
COOKING TIME 10 minutes

1 pound 2 ounce piece of boneless lamb, wrapped and semifrozen 25 minutes (*see page 217*)
2 teaspoons cornstarch
1 tablespoon oyster sauce
2 tablespoons light soy sauce
1 tablespoon dark soy sauce
1 teaspoon sugar
1 tablespoon sunflower oil
1 garlic clove, finely chopped
2 or 3 scallions, cut into pieces 2 inches long
1 red chili, seeded and thinly sliced
1 zucchini, sliced
½ orange, peeled and cut into bite-size pieces
scant ⅔ cup orange juice

TO SERVE
1 recipe quantity Boiled Long-Grain Rice (*see page 214*)

1 Remove the partially frozen lamb fillet from the freezer and discard the plastic wrap. Using a sharp knife, cut the lamb against the grain into ¼-inch slices. Put the lamb in a bowl with the cornstarch, oyster sauce, light and dark soy sauces and sugar, and toss until the pieces of lamb are well coated in the sauce. Set aside.

2 Heat half of the oil in a wok or large skillet over high heat until smoking hot. Tip in the lamb and any liquid, and stir-fry 2 minutes, or until sealed all around. Remove the lamb from the pan, using a slotted spoon, and set aside.

3 Heat the remaining oil in the wok or pan over medium heat, then add the garlic, scallions and chili, and stir-fry 1 to 2 minutes until softened but not browned. Add the zucchini and stir-fry about 1 minute, then return the lamb to the wok or pan and stir-fry 2 minutes longer. Add the orange pieces and juice and bring to a gentle boil for a few seconds. Serve immediately with boiled rice.

cantonese steamed fish

Steaming is one of the most important techniques used in Chinese cooking. It is a very healthy way to cook and retains the flavors of the food, too. A bamboo steamer is ideal, but if you want to steam larger items, such as whole fish, then a wok is handy. In China, the whole fish symbolizes abundance, so serving steamed whole fish is a must during Chinese New Year because it symbolizes a wish for abundance in the New Year.

SERVES 4
PREPARATION TIME 20 minutes, plus 45 minutes soaking and marinating time
COOKING TIME 10 minutes

1 pound 12 ounces whole red snapper, sea bream, sea bass or any other white-flesh fish, scaled and gutted
1 tomato, sliced
1 tablespoon light soy sauce
1 tablespoon oyster sauce
1 tablespoon sesame oil
2 tablespoons Shaoxing rice wine
1-ounce package dried mushrooms, such as shiitake, porcini or Chinese mushrooms, soaked, drained and thinly sliced (*see page 217*)
½-inch piece of ginger-root, peeled and cut into fine matchsticks
2 scallions, cut into matchsticks
freshly ground black pepper

TO SERVE
1 recipe quantity Boiled Long-Grain Rice (*see page 214*)

1 Rinse the fish inside and out under cold running water and pat dry with paper towels. Using a sharp knife, make three diagonal slits on both sides of the fish. Arrange the tomato on the base of a heatproof platter that will fit inside a wok. Lay the fish on top.

2 Mix together the soy sauce, oyster sauce, sesame oil and rice wine in a small bowl and season with pepper. Pour the sauce over the fish and sprinkle with the mushrooms and ginger. Cover with plastic wrap and leave to marinate in the refrigerator about 20 minutes.

3 Place several round cookie cutters or a wire cooling rack with legs at least 1-inch tall inside a wok. Leaving a minimum gap of ½ inch below the steamer, add water to the wok and bring to a boil over medium-high heat. Set the heatproof plate with the fish on the rack and steam, covered tightly with a lid, 10 minutes, or until the flesh separates from the bone easily and looks opaque when a fork is inserted into it. Keep an eye on the level of the water, adding more boiling water if necessary. Two minutes before the end of cooking, sprinkle with the scallions. Serve immediately with boiled rice.

chicken & sticky rice in Lotus Leaves

SERVES 4
PREPARATION TIME about
  1 hour
COOKING TIME 50 to 55 minutes

1 teaspoon sugar
2 tablespoons light soy sauce
1 tablespoon dark soy sauce
1 tablespoon oyster sauce
1 tablespoon sesame oil
¾-inch piece of ginger root,
  peeled and finely grated, pulp
  discarded, reserving the juice
1 tablespoon Shaoxing rice
  wine
1 teaspoon cornstarch
1 pound 5 ounces boneless,
  skinless chicken thighs, cut
  into bite-size pieces
2½ cups jasmine rice, soaked
  30 minutes
1 ounce dried shrimp
1 tablespoon sunflower oil
4 ounces air-dried sausage,
  such as Chinese sausage or
  chorizo, diced (optional)
1-ounce package dried
  mushrooms, such as shiitake,
  porcini or Chinese
  mushrooms, soaked, drained
  and roughly chopped (see
  page 217)
4 dried lotus leaves (optional)
freshly ground black pepper

RICE SEASONING
¼ teaspoon sea salt
1 tablespoon sugar
1 tablespoon light soy sauce
2 tablespoons dark soy sauce
1 tablespoon oyster sauce
2 tablespoons sesame oil

1 Mix the sugar, light and dark soy sauces, oyster sauce, sesame oil,
   ginger juice, rice wine and cornstarch in a large bowl until combined,
   then season with pepper. Add the chicken and toss until each piece
   of chicken is well coated with the marinade. Cover with plastic wrap
   and leave to marinate in the refrigerator at least 2 hours.

2 Drain the soaking rice and transfer to a bowl. Mix all the rice
   seasoning ingredients together, season with pepper and then mix
   through the rice.

3 Place a sheet of wax paper on the base of a bamboo or electric
   steamer and spread the rice mixture out on top. Sprinkle with
   1 tablespoon water, then steam the rice cake 30 minutes, or until
   nicely risen. After 15 minutes, sprinkle with 1 or 2 tablespoons
   more water. Remove the rice cake from the steamer and set aside
   to cool.

4 Meanwhile, put the dried shrimp in a small bowl, cover with water
   and let soak 15 to 20 minutes. Drain well and set aside.

5 Heat the sunflower oil in a skillet over medium-high heat, then add
   the air-dried sausage, if using, and stir-fry 1 minute. Add the
   mushrooms and shrimp and stir-fry 2 minutes. Tip in the marinated
   chicken and cook 5 minutes, or until the chicken starts to turn
   opaque, stirring occasionally. Add 3 tablespoons water and cook
   3 to 4 minutes longer until the chicken starts to turn golden brown.
   Transfer to a bowl and set aside.

6 Fill a large saucepan or wok with water and bring to a boil. Slowly
   submerge the lotus leaves into the water and cook 1 to 2 minutes
   until soft. Refresh under cold running water and pat dry with a dish
   towel. Trim off the hard stems and cut the leaves in quarters.

7 To assemble, layer 2 pieces of the lotus leaf together and spoon
   about 2 heaping tablespoons of rice in the center. Slightly flatten
   the rice, then spread 3 heaped tablespoons of the chicken filling
   evenly over the top. Spoon another heaping tablespoon of rice over
   the chicken. Fold the bottom side of the leaves over the filling, fold
   in the two sides and then roll the package over to enclose the filling.
   Continue with the remaining ingredients to make up 8 packages.
   The packages can also be made with wax paper or foil, if preferred.

8 Arrange the packages in the bamboo or electric steamer and steam
   20 to 25 minutes until cooked through. Make sure that the heat is
   maintained throughout the steaming process. Serve immediately.

CHICKEN & VEGETABLE STEAMED BUNS

I use chicken here, but leftover barbecued or roast pork also works. The buns freeze really well, so if you don't need the full quantity, freeze them unsteamed. All you need to do then for a delicious dim sum in minutes is thaw the buns before steaming.

MAKES 25 small buns
PREPARATION TIME 2 hours
  45 minutes, plus cooling time
COOKING TIME 20 to 30 minutes

1 teaspoon sesame oil
1 tablespoon light soy sauce
1 tablespoon dark soy sauce
1 tablespoon oyster sauce
1 tablespoon Shaoxing
  rice wine
2 teaspoons sugar
½ teaspoon cornstarch
1 tablespoon sesame seeds
12 ounces boneless, skinless
  chicken thighs or chicken
  breast halves, trimmed and
  cut into bite-size pieces
2 tablespoons sunflower oil
2 garlic cloves, finely chopped
½-inch piece of ginger-root,
  peeled and finely chopped
1 carrot, cut into matchsticks
7 ounces Jerusalem artichokes,
  water chestnuts or jicamas,
  peeled and cut into
  matchsticks
2 scallions, finely chopped
freshly ground black pepper

BUN DOUGH
scant ⅓ cup sugar
1 teaspoon Shaoxing rice wine
3¼ cups all-purpose flour, plus
  extra for dusting
2 teaspoons active dried yeast
  granules
2 teaspoons baking powder

1 Combine the sesame oil, light and dark soy sauces, oyster sauce, rice wine, sugar and cornstarch in a large bowl, stirring until the sugar is dissolved. Season with pepper, then add the chicken and toss until each piece of chicken is well coated with the marinade. Cover with plastic wrap and leave to marinate in the refrigerator at least 2 hours.

2 To make the bun dough, mix together the sugar, rice wine and a scant 1¼ cups water until the sugar is dissolved. In a large mixing bowl, combine the flour, yeast and baking powder, and make a well in the center. Slowly pour in the sugared liquid and combine with the flour to form a soft dough.

3 Turn the dough out onto a lightly floured surface and knead 10 minutes or until it is smooth and elastic. Shape the dough into a ball, put in a bowl and cover with a damp dish towel. Set aside in a warm place 45 minutes to 1 hour until it has doubled in size.

4 Heat 1 tablespoon of the sunflower oil in a skillet over medium-high heat. Add the garlic and ginger and cook, stirring occasionally, 1 to 2 minutes until fragrant but not colored. Add the carrot and Jerusalem artichokes and cook 10 minutes. Add 2 tablespoons water and cook 5 to 10 minutes longer until the vegetables have softened. Remove from the heat and set aside to cool.

5 Meanwhile, heat a skillet over medium heat, then add the sesame seeds and dry-roast until fragrant and starting to brown. Remove and set aside. Add the remaining tablespoon of sunflower oil to the skillet over medium-high heat. When the oil is hot, add the marinated chicken and cook 10 to 15 minutes until golden brown and cooked through. Add the toasted sesame seeds, scallions and 1 tablespoon water, and cook 1 minute. Remove from the heat and combine with the carrot and Jerusalem artichoke stir-fry. Let cool.

6 Turn the dough out onto a lightly floured surface and divide in half. Roll each piece of dough into a cylinder, then divide each cylinder into 25 equal portions. Shape the dough portions into balls, covering them with a damp dish towel as you go so they don't dry out. Let rest 15 minutes. Meanwhile, cut up 25 small squares of wax paper for the buns to rest on when they are cooked.

7 Lightly dust the work surface with flour again, then take a dough ball and flatten it with the palm of your hand. Using a rolling pin, roll the dough into a 4-inch disk. Place the disk on the palm of your hand and put 1 heaped tablespoon of the cooled filling in the center. Gather up the edge of the dough around the filling to create a small bag shape. Twist the gathered pleats of dough and pinch them together to seal. Then put the bun on a small square of wax paper, pleat-side up, and cover with a damp dish towel. Repeat to make the remaining buns, then rest about 30 minutes.

8 Keeping the wax paper beneath the buns, arrange them in a bamboo or electric steamer. Leave a space equal to half the size of a bun between each bun so they don't stick together when they expand during cooking. Working in batches, steam the buns 5 to 7 minutes until soft and fluffy to the touch, but not springy. Serve hot.

STEAMED SHRIMP DUMPLINGS

MAKES about 32
PREPARATION TIME 1 hour
30 minutes, plus 1 hour
marinating time
COOKING TIME 15 to 20 minutes

5½ ounces raw, peeled jumbo
  shrimp, deveined and cut
  into small cubes (*see
  page 216*)
¾ ounce bamboo shoots,
  finely chopped
1 teaspoon cornstarch
½ teaspoon sea salt
½ teaspoon sugar
½ teaspoon chicken stock
  granules
½ teaspoon sesame oil
freshly ground black pepper

HAR GOW WRAPPERS
¾ cup wheat starch, plus extra
  for dusting
2 tablespoons cornstarch
¼ teaspoon fine sea salt
3 tablespoons vegetable oil,
  plus extra for oiling

TO SERVE
Chili Oil (*see page 211—
  optional*)

1 Toss the shrimp and bamboo shoots together in a bowl, then add
   the cornstarch and stir in with a wooden spoon. Add the salt, sugar,
   chicken stock granules and sesame oil, and mix until well combined.
   Season with pepper, then cover with plastic wrap and let chill in the
   refrigerater 1 hour.

2 Meanwhile, to make the har gow wrappers, mix together the wheat
   starch, cornstarch and salt in a bowl. Pour in ½ cup boiling water
   and stir with a wooden spoon to form a dough. Cover with a damp
   dish towel and let cool 20 minutes, then add the vegetable oil and
   knead until the dough is very smooth.

3 Roll the dough into a long sausage shape on a lightly floured
   surface, then divide it into 32 equal portions. Shape each portion
   into a ball and flatten slightly between your palms. Place a flattened
   dough ball on an oiled surface or cutting board and, using a rolling
   pin, roll into a 3½-inch disk. Cut the rolled dough into a neat disk
   using a 3¼-inch cookie cutter, then place the wrapper on a large,
   lightly floured cookie sheet. Cover with a damp dish towel while
   you make the remaining wrappers.

4 To assemble the dumplings, place a wrapper on the palm of your
   hand. Spoon 3 or 4 heaping teaspoons of the filling in the center of
   the wrapper and flatten slightly. Fold the lower edge of the wrapper
   over the filling to form a half-moon shape, leaving a small gap at the
   top of the lower half of the wrapper.

5 Pinch the pastry along the curve to seal, then working from one
   corner of the sealed pastry, use your thumb and index finger to fold
   over and pinch the pastry together to form a pleat. Continue to
   work around the edge to the top of the curve, then repeat from the
   other corner. Each side should have 5 or 6 pleats, and the bottom
   underneath the dumpling should remain flat. Press gently into the
   base of the pastry to form a crescent shape, then place the dumpling
   on a lightly oiled plate and cover with a damp dish towel. Repeat for
   the remaining dumplings.

6 Place a sheet of wax paper on the base of a bamboo or electric
   steamer and lightly oil. Arrange about 8 dumplings on the paper,
   leaving a gap between each dumpling so they don't stick together.
   Steam 3 to 4 minutes until cooked through. Repeat until all the
   dumplings are cooked. Serve immediately with chili oil, if liked.

sweet peanut & sesame balls

These little gems are generously coated with sesame seeds and have a gorgeous crispy base. The texture of the pastry is slightly chewy and the filling is smooth with crunchy chunks of peanuts. It's a recipe that remains a favorite in our family.

MAKES 20 to 22
PREPARATION TIME 50 minutes
COOKING TIME 20 to 30 minutes

scant ⅓ cup superfine sugar
heaping 1¾ cups glutinous rice
   flour, plus extra for dusting
scant ⅔ cup skinless raw
   peanuts
heaping ⅓ cup fruit sugar or
   granulated sugar
2 cups sunflower oil, for
   deep-frying
scant ½ cup sesame seeds

1 Add the superfine sugar to 1 cup water and stir until dissolved. Put the rice flour into a large mixing bowl and make a well in the center. Slowly pour in the sugared water and combine with the flour to form a soft dough. Turn the dough out onto a lightly floured surface, roll it into a cylinder and divide into 20 to 22 equal portions.

2 Heat a skillet over medium-high heat, then add the peanuts and dry-roast until fragrant and starting to brown. Remove from the heat and roughly grind in a food processor or blender until you have a fine powder that still has some chunks in it. Tip the ground peanuts into a bowl and add the fruit sugar, 2 tablespoons of the oil and 3 tablespoons water. Stir into a rough paste and set aside.

3 Fill a small bowl with water and pour the sesame seeds onto a small plate. Take a portion of the dough, shape it into a ball and then press into a 3¼-inch disk. Flatten the edges so the center of the disk is slightly thicker. Spoon 1 or 2 heaping teaspoons of the peanut paste into the center of the pastry, gather up the edges and shape into a ball. Repeat for the remaining peanut balls, then dip each ball in the water and coat with the sesame seeds.

4 Heat the oil in a deep, heavy-bottomed saucepan to 325°F, or until a small piece of bread dropped into the oil turns brown after 20 seconds. Gently slide 3 to 4 sesame balls into the oil and fry 3 to 4 minutes until golden brown. Make sure the oil doesn't get too hot, otherwise the sesame seeds will burn. Use a slotted spoon to push the balls down into the oil so they cook evenly. Using the slotted spoon, remove the sesame balls from the oil and drain on paper towels. Repeat until all the balls are cooked. Serve hot or cold.

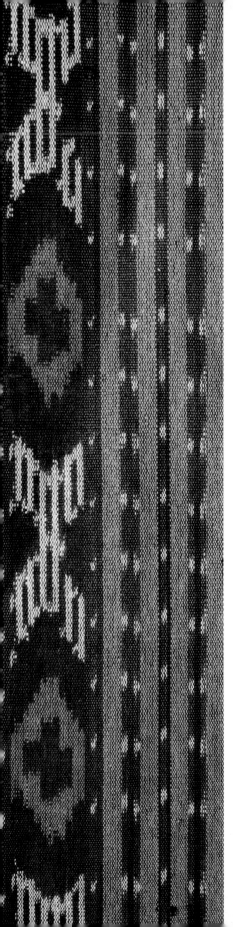

PHILIPPINES & INDONESIA

Filipino cuisine is an exotic fusion of Chinese and Spanish cuisines with hints of influences from the Americas and other Asian countries. A popular dish that demonstrates the Chinese influence is Filipino Shrimp & Pork Noodles (*see page 74*). A modern twist here is the use of saffron threads for coloring instead of the common traditional coloring ingredient, achiote seeds. South American influences can be seen in the dish Citrus-Cured Tuna & Tomato Salad (*see page 78*), which is similar to Ceviche and uses a number of key Filipino ingredients, such as chili, ground coriander, garlic and ginger. A dish like Beef, Peanut & Vegetable Stew (*see page 70*) is a good example of Spanish influence, where the techniques of boiling and braising are used. Other essential ingredients in Filipino cuisine are fish sauce, vinegar, pepper and tamarind.

With more than 18,000 islands, Indonesia is the world's largest archipelago. It has a rich history, which can be seen in its flavorsome cuisine. Indonesian dishes can be hot, sweet, sour and salty, but often have fragrant undertones that come from the use of coconut milk and lemongrass. Both the fresh and dried varieties of turmeric and chili, as well as fresh cilantro and ground coriander, play an important role in Indonesian cooking, as do cumin and pepper. The very popular Balinese Fish Satay (*see page 81*) is an example of good use of these aromatic spices, which may be used also as a rub, such as in Balinese Roast Duck in Banana Leaves (*see page 69*), or combined in spice pastes and used in stir-fries such as Indonesian Chicken Fried Rice (*see page 66*).

indonesian chicken fried rice

SERVES 4

PREPARATION TIME 45 minutes minutes, plus cooking and chilling the rice

COOKING TIME 20 to 25 minutes

1 green bird's-eye chili, seeded and roughly chopped
2 red chilies, seeded and roughly chopped
2 shallots, roughly chopped
3 garlic cloves, roughly chopped
½ teaspoon roasted shrimp paste (*see page 217*)
1 teaspoon grated palm sugar or soft light brown sugar
2¼ ounces dried anchovies
2 tablespoons sunflower oil
7 ounces skinless, boneless chicken breast halves, cut into bite-size pieces
2¾ ounces finely sliced green beans
1 recipe quantity Boiled Long-Grain Rice, cooked the night before and chilled (*see page 214*)
2 tablespoons light soy sauce
2 tablespoons dark soy sauce
1 tablespoon liquid honey
1 small handful of cilantro leaves, finely chopped
sea salt

TO SERVE
1 handful of Indonesian shrimp crackers (krupuk)
Sambal (*see page 213*)

1 Put the green bird's-eye chili, red chilies, shallots, garlic and shrimp paste in a mortar and pestle or a food processor and blend to a smooth paste. Transfer to a bowl and add a pinch of salt and the sugar. Mix well and set aside.

2 Soak the dried anchovies in water 1 to 2 minutes, then drain and pat dry with paper towels, squeezing out any excess liquid. Heat 1 tablespoon of the oil in a skillet over medium-high heat. Add the anchovies and stir-fry 1 to 2 minutes until golden brown. Set aside.

3 Heat the remaining tablespoon of oil in a wok or large skillet over high heat until smoking hot. Add the chili paste and stir-fry 3 to 4 minutes until fragrant. Tip in the chicken pieces and stir-fry 5 minutes, or until cooked through and starting to turn golden. Add the sliced green beans and cook about 3 minutes, or until tender.

4 Add the boiled rice, break up any lumps and stir-fry 5 to 10 minutes until the chicken is cooked and the rice is hot. Add the light and dark soy sauces and honey, and mix in well. Tip in the fried anchovies and chopped cilantro, and stir until well combined. Serve immediately with the shrimp crackers and Sambal on the side.

Balinese Roast Duck in Banana Leaves

SERVES 4 to 6
PREPARATION TIME 20 minutes, plus minimum 3 hours marinating time
COOKING TIME 2 hours

4-pound duck
enough banana leaves or foil for wrapping

MARINADE
10 shallots, roughly chopped
6 garlic cloves, roughly chopped
2 crushed lemongrass stalks, outer leaves discarded and ends trimmed, roughly chopped
4 fresh lime leaves, roughly chopped
1½-inch piece of ginger-root, peeled and roughly chopped
5 red chilies, seeded and roughly chopped
2 green bird's-eye chilies, seeded and roughly chopped
2 teaspoons roasted shrimp paste (*see page 217*)
½ teaspoon black peppercorns
4 macadamia nuts
¾-inch piece of fresh turmeric, peeled and roughly chopped or 1 teaspoon ground turmeric
1 teaspoon ground coriander
½ teaspoon ground cumin
1 teaspoon sea salt
1 teaspoon honey
1 tablespoon lime juice

TO SERVE
1 recipe quantity Boiled Long-Grain Rice (*see page 214*)

1 Rinse the duck thoroughly inside and out under cold running water and pat dry inside and out with paper towels. Lightly prick the skin all over with a fork.

2 Put all the marinade ingredients in a food processor, except the ground turmeric, if using, coriander, cumin, salt, honey and lime juice and blend to a smooth paste. Transfer to a small bowl and stir in the remaining ingredients. Rub the duck inside and out with the marinade until it is well coated. Layer the banana leaves or foil on a large plate, set the duck on top and wrap it in the banana leaves or foil. Secure with toothpicks, if necessary. Cover with plastic wrap and leave to marinate in the refrigerator 3 to 4 hours or, for an even better flavor, overnight.

3 Heat the oven to 400°F. Put a wire rack in a roasting pan and set the duck on the rack. Place on the middle shelf of the oven and roast 15 minutes. Reduce the temperature to 350°F and continue to cook 1½ to 2 hours until the juices run clear when you insert the tip of a sharp knife into the thickest part of the duck.

4 Unwrap the duck then, using a sharp carving knife, slice the meat into pieces. Serve hot with boiled rice.

beef, peanut & vegetable stew

Here is a hearty dish that doesn't require expensive ingredients and is quick to prepare, but it does need some patience while it simmers away to allow the meat to tenderize and the flavors to develop. Traditionally, this Filipino stew is made with oxtail, a variety of vegetables and a peanut-spice paste. Instead, I have used chuck steak cut into bite-size pieces and dry-fried, and ground peanuts.

SERVES 6
PREPARATION TIME 15 minutes
COOKING TIME about 2 hours
   30 minutes

1 cup skinless raw peanuts
3 pounds 5 ounces to 4 pounds
   chuck steak, fat trimmed, cut
   into
   bite-size pieces
1 tablespoon sunflower oil
a large pinch of saffron threads
2 onions, roughly chopped
8 garlic cloves, chopped
1 recipe quantity Kare Kare
   Spice Paste (*see page 207*)
7 ounces trimmed green beans,
   sliced into 2½-inch pieces
1 medium eggplant, cut into
   bite-size pieces
7 ounces baby carrots,
   trimmed
2 tablespoons lime juice or
   1 recipe quantity Tamarind
   Water (*see page 217*)
sea salt

TO SERVE
1 recipe quantity Boiled
   Long-Grain Rice
   (*see page 214*)

1 Heat a skillet over medium-high heat, then add the peanuts and dry-roast until fragrant and starting to brown. Remove from the heat and roughly grind the peanuts in a food processor or blender until you have a fine powder that still has some chunks in it. Set aside.

2 Rinse the beef under cold running water and pat dry with paper towels. Heat the oil in a large flameproof Dutch oven over medium-high heat, then add half the chuck steak and stir-fry 4 to 5 minutes until beginning to brown. Remove from the pan, using a slotted spoon, and drain on paper towels. Repeat with the remaining steak, adding more oil as required.

3 Mix together the saffron and 2 tablespoons warm water in a small bowl and set aside. Place the Dutch oven back over medium-high heat, then add the onions and garlic, and stir-fry 2 minutes, or until soft and translucent. Add the spice paste, stirring occasionally, 10 to 15 minutes until fragrant and the oil starts to rise to the surface, then stir in the browned steak and combine well. Add the saffron and the soaking liquid and pour in a scant 1¼ cups water. Bring to a boil, cover with a tight-fitting lid, reduce the heat to low and simmer about 1 hour, skimming off any scum that rises to the surface from time to time.

4 After 1 hour of cooking, tip the ground peanuts, sliced green beans, eggplant, carrots and lime juice into the stew and season with salt. Give it a good stir to coat the vegetables evenly with the mixture, replace the lid and continue to simmer at least 1 hour longer, or until the beef is almost falling apart and the sauce has thickened. Serve immediately with boiled rice.

makassar beef soup

This soup originates from the island of Sulawesi, Indonesia. It is wonderfully aromatic, with the citrus of the lemongrass and earthiness of spices balancing the richness of the beef perfectly. To make a substantial meal, you can serve it with rice noodles.

SERVES 4 to 6
PREPARATION TIME 30 minutes, plus 10 minutes cooling time
COOKING TIME about 1 hour

1 pound 2 ounce piece of beef tenderloin or fillet
¼ teaspoon white peppercorns
1 tablespoon sugar
2 crushed lemongrass stalks, outer leaves discarded and ends trimmed
1 onion, sliced
2 teaspoons lime juice
2 tablespoons sunflower oil
1 recipe quantity Coto Makassar Spice Paste (*see page 207*)
2 scallions, finely chopped
1 small handful of cilantro leaves, chopped
1 small handful of mint leaves, chopped
2 tablespoons Fried Shallot (*see page 212*)

TO SERVE
14 ounces cooked rice noodles (*see page 215*)

1 Place the beef on a cutting board and trim off the fat. Remove any silver skin by slipping the knife between the meat and the skin. Slide the blade along the beef and pull away the silver skin until it is all removed.

2 Put the beef, white peppercorns, sugar, lemongrass, onion and 2 quarts water in a very large saucepan over high heat and bring to a boil. Skim any scum from the surface, then reduce the heat to low and simmer gently 30 minutes.

3 Remove the beef from the stock and set aside 5 to 10 minutes to cool. Using a sharp knife, cut the tenderloin or fillet into strips ⅛ inch thick. Return the meat pieces to the stock, add the lime juice and continue to simmer 15 to 20 minutes.

4 Meanwhile, heat the oil in a very large skillet over medium-high heat. Add the spice paste and cook gently, stirring occasionally, 10 to 15 minutes until fragrant and the oil starts to rise to the surface. Pour in the stock and beef, and simmer 10 to 15 minutes until the beef is tender.

5 Serve immediately with rice noodles, sprinkled with the chopped scallions, cilantro, mint and fried shallots.

shrimp & tamarind soup

This Filipino soup is rich in color and flavor. When I first tasted some, it reminded me of the tangy spiciness of Shrimp Tom Yum Soup (*see page 135*). This made me think how a lot of Southeast Asian food shares many similarities. Traditionally, water spinach is used in this recipe, but I have substituted baby spinach leaves instead.

SERVES 4 to 6
PREPARATION TIME 15 minutes
COOKING TIME 20 minutes

1 pound 12 ounces raw,
  unpeeled jumbo shrimp
2 shallots, quartered
2 green bird's-eye chilies,
  whole
3½ ounces green beans sliced
  into 2-inch pieces
2 tomatoes, skinned and
  quartered (*see page 217*)
1 recipe quantity Tamarind
  Water (*see page 217*)
2 teaspoons sugar
juice of 1 lime
5½ ounces baby spinach leaves
sea salt

TO SERVE
14 ounces cooked rice noodles
  (*see page 215*)

1 Using a pair of poultry shears, trim off each shrimp the feelers, rostrum, legs and the sharp end of the tail. Make a slit along the back of the shrimp with a sharp knife and pull out the black vein with the tip of the knife or your fingers. Rinse the shrimp under cold running water and pat dry with paper towels.

2 Bring 1½ quarts water to a boil in a large saucepan over medium-high heat. Add the shallots and chilies, and cook 2 minutes, then add the green beans and cook 1 to 2 minutes longer. Reduce the heat to low, add the tomatoes and simmer 2 minutes or until the tomatoes begin to soften.

3 Add the shrimp and cook, covered, 4 to 5 minutes until they turn pink and are cooked through. Add the tamarind water and sugar, then season with salt and add the lime juice, to taste. Bring back to a boil for a few seconds, then add the spinach and cook 1 minute, or until it starts to wilt. Serve immediately with rice noodles.

FILIPINO SHRIMP & PORK NOODLES

Originally introduced by the Chinese, noodle dishes are a household staple in almost all Filipino homes. In the Chinese culture, noodles symbolize longevity, so this dish, which is also a very colorful and festive dish, is a popular choice to serve at birthday celebrations.

SERVES 4 to 6
PREPARATION TIME 25 minutes
COOKING TIME about
    30 minutes

9 ounces raw, peeled jumbo
    shrimp, heads removed, with
    tails left on and deveined
    (*see page 216*)
2 tablespoons sunflower oil
3½ ounces firm tofu, cut
    into ¾-inch cubes
3½ ounces ground pork
2 teaspoons cornstarch
a pinch of saffron threads
3 tablespoons fish sauce
1 teaspoon sugar
7 ounces rice vermicelli,
    soaked according to the
    package directions
3 hard-boiled eggs, cut into
    wedges
2 tablespoons Fried Shallots
    (*see page 212*)
2 scallions, sliced into fine
    strips lengthwise
2¾ ounces toasted dried
    anchovies (*see page 217—
    optional*)
sea salt and freshly ground
    black pepper

TO SERVE
1 lime, cut into wedges

1 Pour 1 cup water into a large saucepan and bring to a boil over medium-high heat. Tip in the shrimp and cook until they turn pink and are cooked through. Using a slotted spoon, remove the shrimp and keep warm. Reserve the water.

2 Heat 1 tablespoon of the oil in a skillet over medium-high heat. Add the tofu and stir-fry 2 to 3 minutes until golden brown and crisp. Remove from the pan and set aside.

3 Reduce the heat to medium and add the remaining 1 tablespoon of oil to the pan. When the oil is hot, add the ground pork, breaking up any lumps. Increase the heat to high and cook 5 to 10 minutes, stirring frequently. Meanwhile, mix together the cornstarch and 1 tablespoon water in a small bowl.

4 Pour the reserved liquid from the shrimp into the pan and bring to a boil over high heat a few seconds, then reduce the heat to medium-low. Add the saffron, fish sauce and sugar, and season with salt and pepper. Stir in the cornstarch mixture and bring back to a gentle boil. Reduce the heat to low and simmer for 5 minutes.

5 Meanwhile, bring plenty of water to a boil in a large saucepan. Drain the soaking rice vermicelli and add to the pan. Cook 2 to 3 minutes until softened. Drain the noodles well and place on a serving plate.

6 Bring the simmering sauce to a boil a few seconds and then remove from the heat. Ladle the sauce over the noodles and divide the fried tofu, shrimp and hard-boiled eggs into the bowls. Sprinkle with the fried shallots, scallions and anchovies, if using. Serve immediately with lime wedges.

gado gado

The main feature of Gado Gado, a popular Indonesian vegetable salad, is the peanut sauce, which transforms all the simple ingredients into a harmonious bowl of flavors. And to give it additional crunch, krupuk (Indonesian shrimp crackers), are served sprinkled on the top or left whole on the side. This salad works well with all kinds of vegetables, so feel free to experiment.

SERVES 4
PREPARATION TIME 1 hour
COOKING TIME about
   30 minutes

1 cup skinless raw peanuts
3 tablespoons sunflower oil
1 recipe quantity Gado Gado
   Spice Paste (*see page 207*)
1 tablespoon lime juice or
   ½ recipe quantity Tamarind
   Water (*see page 217*)
2 tablespoons sugar
3½ ounces firm tofu, sliced
5½ ounces trimmed green
   beans, cut into 2½in pieces
5½ ounces bean sprouts or
   edamame (soy) beans
1 small cucumber, halved
   lengthwise, seeded and sliced
   into chunks
1 small carrot, cut into
   matchsticks
2 hard-boiled eggs, halved
sea salt

TO SERVE
1 handful of Indonesian
   shrimp crackers (krupuk)

1 Set a skillet over medium-high heat, then add the peanuts and dry-roast until fragrant and starting to brown. Remove from the heat and roughly grind the peanuts in a food processor or blender until you have a fine powder still with some chunks. Set aside.

2 Heat 1 tablespoon of the oil in a skillet over medium-high heat, then add the spice paste and cook, stirring occasionally, 10 to 15 minutes until fragrant and the oil starts to rise to the surface. Add the lime juice, sugar and 1 cup water, then season with salt. Tip in the ground peanuts and stir to combine. Bring to a boil, then remove from the heat and keep warm.

3 Meanwhile, add the remaining 2 tablespoons of oil to a skillet over medium-high heat. Add the tofu pieces and shallow-fry for 3 to 4 minutes until golden brown on all sides. Remove the tofu with a slotted spoon and drain on paper towels. Set aside.

4 Bring a large saucepan of water to a boil, then tip in the green beans and cook 3 to 4 minutes until tender but still crunchy. Remove from the water with a slotted spoon, refresh under cold running water and set aside. Bring the water back to a boil, add the bean sprouts and cook about 20 seconds. Drain and set aside. Serve hot with Indonesian prawn crackers.

CITRUS-CURED Tuna & TOMaTO SaLaD

Known as Kinilaw in the Philippines, this dish is similar to Ceviche and is usually served as a side dish. The combination of raw fish with all the other aromatic ingredients makes it a very refreshing appetizer, especially during the summer months. Vinegar is often used to partially cook the fish, but I have substituted it with lime and lemon juice because I love the freshness they bring to the dish.

SERVES 4
PREPARATION TIME 20 minutes, plus 25 minutes curing time

1 pound 2 ounces skinless, boneless tuna steaks
2 tablespoons lime juice
2 tablespoons lemon juice
2 teaspoons sugar
1 garlic clove, grated
¼-inch piece of ginger-root, peeled and grated
1 green bird's-eye chili, seeded and finely diced
1 small red onion, finely chopped
2 scallions, finely sliced
8 cherry tomatoes, quartered
1 small handful of cilantro leaves, roughly chopped
sea salt and freshly ground black pepper

1 Place the tuna on a cutting board and cut it against the grain into ¼-inch slices. Put in a bowl, season with salt and pepper, and set aside.

2 Mix the lime juice, lemon juice, sugar and a pinch of salt in a small bowl until the sugar is dissolved. Stir in the garlic, ginger, chili and onion, then pour the sauce over the tuna slices. Toss the tuna until well coated with the dressing, cover with plastic wrap and leave to marinate in the refrigerator about 10 minutes.

3 Remove the tuna from the fridge and add the scallions and cherry tomatoes to the bowl. Return to the fridge to marinate 5 minutes longer, then remove and let stand at room temperature 10 minutes longer. Sprinkle with the chopped cilantro before serving.

Balinese Fish Satay

These satays are great served as party food. They offer something different from the usual beef or chicken satay and are delicious served with Sambal Matah (a Balinese Sambal that is unique because the ingredients are sliced instead of ground to a paste).

MAKES 16
PREPARATION TIME 45 minutes
COOKING TIME about 45 minutes

1 pound 4 ounces skinless, boneless white fish fillets
1 recipe quantity Sate Lilit Ikan Spice Paste (*see page 209*)
¼ cup freshly grated coconut (*see page 216*) or dry unsweetened shredded coconut
1 tablespoon honey
16 lemongrass stalks, outer leaves discarded and ends trimmed
1 tablespoon sunflower oil, plus extra for greasing
sea salt

TO SERVE
Sambal Matah (*see page 213*)

1 Cut the fish fillets into chunky pieces, then transfer to a food processor. Blend to a smooth paste then scrape into a bowl using a spatula. Add the spice paste, coconut, honey and a pinch of salt to the bowl and mix until thoroughly combined.

2 Prepare a bowl of slightly salted water. Moisten one hand with the salted water then gather up the fish paste and shape into a ball. Pick up the ball, then slam it down into the bowl a few times, or until the mixture is glossy and the texture is smooth and springy. Remoisten your hand as necessary.

3 Place 2 heaped tablespoons of the mixture into the center of your moistened palm. Use the back of the spoon to flatten the mixture into a 2-inch circle, then slightly close your hand and place the root end of a lemongrass stalk onto the mixture. Mold the paste around the lemongrass, covering only half the stick and place on a plate. Repeat until all the ingredients are used, then brush the fish satay with oil until coated all around.

4 Pour some oil into a cast iron grill pan or large, heavy-bottomed skillet over medium-high heat, then use paper towels to grease the pan evenly and soak up any excess oil. Grill a batch of 5 or 6 satays 7 to 10 minutes on each side until golden brown and cooked through. Transfer to a serving plate and keep warm. Grease the pan again, if required, and repeat until all the satays are cooked. Serve hot with the Sambal Matah.

SPICY TOFU

It couldn't be simpler to make this Indonesian-style street food. This snack, which originates from western Java, is served with a pungent, sweet, sour and spicy sauce. It is simply irresistible. For an authentic Javanese experience, you could replace the firm tofu with tofu puffs, which can be found in Asian supermarkets. They provide a crunchy layer while their spongy center soaks up all the flavors.

SERVES 4
PREPARATION TIME 20 minutes
COOKING TIME 20 minutes

1 cup sunflower oil
12 ounces firm tofu, cut into
  bite-size cubes
1 small cucumber, halved
  lengthwise, seeded and sliced
  into chunks

DRESSING
3 shallots, sliced
2 red bird's-eye chilies, seeded
  and chopped
2 green bird's-eye chilies,
  seeded and chopped
1 garlic clove, finely chopped
3 tablespoons grated palm
  sugar or soft light brown
  sugar
2 tablespoons lime juice or
  1 recipe quantity Tamarind
  Water (*see page 217*)

1 To make the dressing, put the shallots, red and green chilies and garlic in a mortar or food processor and pound with a pestle or blend into a rough paste. Transfer to a bowl. In a separate bowl, mix together the sugar with 2 tablespoons hot water until dissolved. Stir in the lime juice and then the prepared chili paste. Set aside.

2 Heat the oil in a deep, heavy-bottomed saucepan or wok to 350°F, or until a small piece of bread dropped into the oil turns brown after 15 seconds. Gently slide the tofu into the oil and fry in batches 10 minutes, or until lightly golden brown. Remove the tofu from the oil, using a slotted spoon, and drain on paper towels. Divide the tofu and cucumber onto four plates and drizzle with the dressing before serving at room temperature.

ɪnᴅonᴇsɪan swᴇᴇᴛ crêpes

Known as martabak manis, these crêpes can be savory or sweet. This sweet version calls for coconut milk, which makes the crêpes both fragrant and light. For a less traditional version, you could fill them with chocolate chips, fruit or anything else you'd like.

MAKES 5 to 6
PREPARATION TIME 20 minutes, plus 25 to 30 minutes resting time
COOKING TIME 45 minutes

scant ⅔ cup self-rising flour
scant ⅓ cup rice flour
1 teaspoon baking powder
½ teaspoon active dried yeast granules
scant ½ cup superfine sugar
1 egg
½ cup coconut milk

FILLING
½ cup raw cashews
scant ¼ cup butter or margarine, slightly softened and cut into cubes, plus extra for greasing
¼ cup fruit sugar or granulated sugar
1 cup dry unsweetened shredded coconut

1 Combine the self-rising flour, rice flour, baking powder, dried active yeast granules and superfine sugar in a mixing bowl. Crack in the egg and stir until combined. In a separate pitcher or bowl, mix together the coconut milk and ⅓ cup 2 tablespoons water, then slowly pour into the dry ingredients. Mix to a smooth batter then set aside at room temperature 25 to 30 minutes.

2 Meanwhile, heat a skillet over medium-high heat, then add the cashews and dry-roast until fragrant and starting to brown. Remove from the heat and roughly grind in a food processor or blender until you have a fine powder that still has some chunks.

3 Lightly grease a 7-inch heavy-bottomed skillet with butter and then set it over medium heat. Spoon a ladleful of the batter into the center of the pan, then swirl the pan to cover the base with the batter. Cook the crêpe 3 to 4 minutes until little bubbles start to form on the surface.

4 Spread a knob of the butter over the crêpe, then sprinkle with 2 teaspoons of the granulated sugar, 1 tablespoon of the ground cashews and 1 tablespoon of the shredded coconut. Use a spatula to check if the crêpe is golden brown underneath, then transfer to a plate and fold it in half. Set aside and keep warm while you make the remaining 4 or 5 crêpes. Serve hot.

steameᴅ rice cakes

Steamed Rice Cakes, known as Puto, are a traditional Filipino dessert. The most popular natural coloring for these is extract of pandan leaves, which gives a bright green color and sweet fragrance. However, I've used green tea powder because it is much easier to work with. Steamed rice cakes are often enjoyed as an afternoon snack with a cup of tea or coffee, but are also often served at breakfast.

MAKES 12
PREPARATION TIME 20 minutes, plus 30 minutes resting time
COOKING TIME 15 minutes

1⅔ cups rice flour
1¼ cups self-rising flour
1 tablespoon baking powder
1 teaspoon dried active yeast granules
heaping ¾ cup sugar
a pinch of sea salt
1¾ cups coconut milk
1½ teaspoons green tea powder
2 tablespoons freshly grated coconut (*see page 216*) or dry unsweetened shredded coconut, to serve
grated jaggery or soft light brown sugar, to serve (optional)

1 Combine the rice flour, self-rising flour, baking powder, dried active yeast granules, sugar and salt in a mixing bowl. Add the coconut milk and 3 tablespoons water, and stir until the sugar has dissolved. Pour half the mixture into a separate bowl, add the green tea powder and mix well. Leave both the green and white mixtures to stand at room temperature 30 minutes.

2 Divide the green mixture into the cups of a six-cup muffin pan or into six ⅓-cup ramekins. Set the muffin pan or ramekins in a bamboo or electric steamer and steam 15 minutes, or until the cakes are nicely risen. Depending on the size of the steamer, you may need to cook the rice cakes in batches. Remove the green steamed rice cakes from the muffin pan or ramekins and repeat with the white mixture to give a total of 12 rice cakes.

3 Sprinkle with coconut and dust with grated jaggery or soft light brown sugar, if liked, before serving hot or cold.

MALAYSIA & SINGAPORE

Malaysian food is like an array of delicious foods that reflects the country's different ethnic backgrounds— Malay, Chinese, Indian, Nyonya, Eurasian and the indigenous people of Borneo. As a result, the cuisine features a wide and varied array of delicious foods. Beef Rendang (*see page 100*) is a perfect example of harmoniously blended Indian and Malaysian cuisines, whereas the spicy, sweet, sour and salty flavors of Penang Assam Laksa (*see page 102*) fuse together Nyonya, Chinese and Malay ingredients and cooking techniques. To add to this variety, many exotic spices brought to Malaysia in the fifteenth century, including cardamom, cinnamon, clove and star anise, are all still popular today, and are used to make Malaysian Chicken Red Curry (*see page 92*).

Singapore was an important port for the spice trade during the British occupation (1819 to 1942), and this, along with the presence of different ethnic groups living there, has resulted in a richly varied food culture. Along with the different spices used, such as cinnamon, coriander, cumin, fennel and five-spice powder, other flavorings often found in this cuisine are chili, ginger, garlic, shallots, soy sauce and shrimp paste, as seen in the mouthwatering Singaporean Chili Crab (*see page 109*). Another dish that provides an all-round example of the flavors and style of Singaporean food, and the strong influence of Chinese cuisine, is Pork & Mushroom Noodles (*see page 96*).

claypot chicken rice

**If you can, cook this dish the traditional way in a claypot.
You will get to enjoy the particularly crunchy layer of rice that
forms at the bottom, a unique characteristic of the dish.
The amazing combination of fluffy yet crunchy rice, chicken
generously coated in a tasty sauce and the earthy flavor of
Chinese mushrooms all make this a mouthwatering dish.**

SERVES 4
PREPARATION TIME 20 minutes,
plus 40 minutes marinating and
soaking time
COOKING TIME 30 to 35 minutes

1 pound 9 ounces chicken
drumsticks or 1 pound
2 ounces skinless, boneless
chicken thighs, cut into
bite-size pieces
1 tablespoon sesame oil
1 tablespoon oyster sauce
2 tablespoons light soy sauce
2 tablespoons dark soy sauce
1 tablespoon Shaoxing rice
wine
1 tablespoon honey
1¼-inch piece of ginger-root,
peeled and finely grated, pulp
discarded, reserving the juice
1¾ cups long-grain rice,
soaked and rested
(*see page 214*)
2 tablespoons sunflower oil
4 dried Chinese mushrooms,
soaked, drained and sliced
into thin strips (*see page 217*)
2 scallions, finely sliced
freshly ground black pepper
2 red bird's-eye chilies, finely
sliced, to serve (optional)

1 If using chicken drumsticks, rinse them under cold running water
and pat dry with paper towels. Remove the skin and then, using
a large chef's knife, cut each drumstick into 2 pieces through the
bone. Put the drumstick pieces or thighs, if using, into a large bowl
and add the sesame oil, oyster sauce, light and dark soy sauces, rice
wine, honey and ginger juice. Season with pepper, then toss until
each piece of chicken is well coated with the marinade. Cover
with plastic wrap and leave to marinate at room temperature
30 minutes.

2 Put the rice in a claypot or deep, heavy-bottomed saucepan placed
over high heat. Pour in 2 cups water and bring to a boil. Stir well,
then reduce the heat to low, cover and simmer 10 minutes.

3 Meanwhile, heat the sunflower oil in a skillet over medium-high
heat. Add the mushrooms and stir-fry 1 minute, then remove with
a slotted spoon and set aside. Add the marinated chicken to the pan,
reserving the marinade, and cook, stirring occasionally, 10 to 12
minutes until browned and almost cooked. Remove from the heat
and set aside.

4 After the rice has simmered 10 minutes and the liquid is almost
absorbed, spread the chicken pieces and mushrooms on top of the
rice. Cover and continue to cook over very low heat 15 minutes
longer, or until the chicken is cooked through. Add the reserved
marinade and cook 4 to 5 minutes, then add the scallions and cook
1 minute longer. Serve immediately with the chilies sprinkled over,
if liked.

Hainanese Chicken Rice

SERVES 4 to 6
PREPARATION TIME 1 hour
15 minutes
COOKING TIME 45 minutes

3 pounds 5 ounces chicken
1 tablespoon sunflower oil
¾-inch piece of ginger root,
    peeled and finely chopped
1 garlic clove, finely chopped
2 shallots, thinly sliced
½ teaspoon sea salt
1¾ cups long-grain rice,
    soaked and rested
3 crushed lemongrass stalks,
    outer leaves discarded and
    ends trimmed
1 scallion, finely chopped, to
    serve
1 small cucumber, halved
    lengthwise, seeded and
    sliced, to serve

CHILI DIPPING SAUCE
5 large red chilies, roughly
    chopped
2 red bird's-eye chilies, seeded
    and roughly chopped
3 garlic cloves, roughly
    chopped
½-inch piece of ginger-root,
    peeled and grated
1¼ tablespoons sugar
2 tablespoons light soy sauce
½ teaspoon sea salt
2 tablespoons lime juice

BASIL DIPPING SAUCE
small handful Thai basil leaves
1 green bird's-eye chili, seeded
    and roughly chopped
4 garlic cloves, roughly
    chopped
1 teaspoon sunflower oil
sea salt

1 To make the chili dipping sauce, put the chilies, garlic and ginger into a food processor and blend to a smooth paste. Transfer to a small bowl, add the sugar and stir until dissolved. Stir in the soy sauce, salt and lime juice and set aside.

2 To make the basil dipping sauce, put the Thai basil leaves, chili and garlic into a food processor and blend to a smooth paste. Transfer to a small bowl, add a pinch of salt and stir in the oil. Set aside.

3 Rinse the chicken thoroughly inside and out under cold running water and pat dry inside and out with paper towels.

4 Half fill a large, heavy-bottomed saucepan with water, and bring to a boil over high heat. Add the chicken, breast-side down, and boil about 20 seconds. Reduce the heat to low, cover and simmer 15 minutes. Skim any scum or fat from the surface, turn over the chicken, cover again and continue to simmer 10 to 15 minutes until the juices run clear when the tip of a sharp knife is inserted into the thickest part of the chicken.

5 Remove the chicken from the stock and set aside until it is cool enough to handle. Leave the chicken stock in the saucepan but turn off the heat. Using a pair of poultry shears or a large sharp knife, cut the chicken into 12 or up to 18 pieces, as preferred.

6 Meanwhile, heat the oil in a saucepan over medium-high heat. Add the ginger, garlic and shallots, and cook, stirring occasionally, 5 to 7 minutes until fragrant but not colored. Add the salt and rice and stir-fry 1 to 2 minutes. Pour in scant 2 cups of the chicken stock and add the lemongrass. Bring to a boil, then stir with a wooden spoon to prevent the rice from sticking to the bottom of the pan. Reduce the heat to low, cover and let simmer gently 20 minutes.

7 Remove the pan from the heat but keep the lid tightly closed. Set aside to steam 10 to 15 minutes until cooked. Fluff up the rice with a fork and discard the lemongrass. Meanwhile, bring the remaining chicken stock to a boil.

8 Divide the rice into individual bowls and top with the chicken pieces. Ladle in the chicken stock. Sprinkle with the chopped scallions before serving with the cucumber, chili dipping sauce and basil dipping sauce on the side.

CHICKEN & SHRIMP LAKSA

SERVES 4 to 6
PREPARATION TIME 45 minutes
COOKING TIME 1 hour
30 minutes, plus cooking the
noodles

1 pound 5 ounces skinless
chicken drumsticks, fat
trimmed
1 pound 2 ounces raw, peeled
jumbo shrimp, deveined
(*see page 216*)
2 tablespoons sunflower oil
2 sprigs curry leaves, roughly
chopped (optional)
1 recipe quantity Laksa Spice
Paste (*see page 206*)
2 cups coconut milk
10½ ounces cooked fresh egg
noodles or 9 ounces dried
fine egg noodles
(*see page 215*)
7 ounces cooked dried rice
vermicelli (*see page 215*)
3½ ounces Chinese long beans
or trimmed green beans,
cut into 2-inch pieces
7 ounces bean sprouts
7 ounces firm tofu, fried
2 hard-boiled eggs, quartered
sea salt

TO SERVE
Chili Paste (*see page 212—
optional*)

1 Pour 6 cups water into a large, heavy-bottomed saucepan and bring
to a boil over medium-high heat. Add the chicken drumsticks and
boil 10 minutes, then reduce the heat to low, cover and simmer 10
minutes. Skim off any scum or fat from the surface and continue to
simmer 10 to 15 minutes until the juices run clear when the tip of a
sharp knife is inserted into the thickest part of the meat. Remove the
drumsticks, using a pair of long-handled tongs, and set aside until
cool enough to touch. Leave the chicken stock simmering in the
saucepan.

2 Strip the meat off of the drumsticks, then shred or slice the meat.
Cover with plastic wrap and set aside. Return the bones to the
stock and continue to simmer 30 minutes.

3 Meanwhile, transfer scant 1¼ cups of the chicken stock into a
separate saucepan and bring to a boil over medium-high heat. Add
the shrimp and cook until they turn pink and are cooked through.
Using a slotted spoon, remove the shrimp from the stock, drain on
paper towels and set aside. Return the shrimp-flavored stock to the
main pan of simmering chicken stock.

4 Heat the oil in a skillet over medium-high heat. Add the curry
leaves, if using, and fry 1 to 2 minutes until fragrant. Add the spice
paste and cook gently, stirring occasionally, 10 to 15 minutes until
fragrant and the oil starts to rise to the surface. Remove the curry
leaves from the pan, then stir the paste into the stock. Add the
coconut milk to the stock, season with salt and stir.

5 Divide the warm, cooked egg noodles and rice vermicelli into
deep soup bowls. Bring a saucepan of water to a boil and blanch
the Chinese long beans 1 minute then, using long-handled
tongs, remove the beans and divide into the bowls of noodles.
Return the water to a boil and blanch the bean sprouts about
20 seconds. Drain and divide into the bowls with the noodles
and beans.

6 Divide the shredded chicken, shrimp, tofu and hard-cooked eggs
into the bowls on top of the bean sprouts. Bring the stock to a
vigorous boil, then ladle into serving bowls. Serve immediately
with chili paste on the side, if liked.

malaysian chicken red curry

When I was learning to cook, my mom shared a tip with me, which she said would ensure my aromatic curries would always be a success. She advised me to use "empat sekawan" (star anise, green cardamom, clove and cinnamon), also known as the Four Buddies. Used here with the spice paste, I guarantee this will be one of the most aromatic red curries you will ever eat.

SERVES 4 to 6
PREPARATION TIME 45 minutes, plus 2 hours 30 minutes marinating and resting time
COOKING TIME 2 hours 15 minutes

2 pounds 4 ounces skinless chicken drumsticks, fat trimmed
1 tablespoon turmeric
2 cups sunflower oil, for deep-frying, plus extra for shallow frying
2 red onions, sliced into rings
4 green cardamom pods
2 star anise
2 cloves
2½-inch cinnamon stick
1 recipe quantity Ayam Masak Merah Spice Paste (*see page 206*)
4 tomatoes, skinned and quartered (*see page 217*)
2 tablespoons lime juice or 1 recipe quantity Tamarind Water (*see page 217*)
2 tablespoons tomato paste
3 tablespoons tomato ketchup
1 teaspoon dark soy sauce
3 tablespoons sugar
sea salt

TO SERVE
1 recipe quantity Boiled Long-Grain Rice (*see page 214*—optional)

1 Season the chicken drumsticks with salt and lightly coat with the turmeric. Cover with plastic wrap and leave to marinate in the refrigerator about 2 hours.

2 Remove the chicken from the refrigerator and leave to stand at room temperature about 30 minutes before deep-frying. Heat the 2 cups of sunflower oil in a wok or deep, heavy-bottomed saucepan to 350°F, or until a small piece of bread dropped into the oil turns brown in 15 seconds. Fry the chicken drumsticks 15 minutes, or until they turn golden brown. Work in batches and don't overcrowd the wok or pan—this will lower the temperature of the oil. Remove the drumsticks from the oil with long-handled tongs and drain on paper towels or a wire rack and set aside.

3 Heat the remaining oil in a saucepan over medium heat. Add the onions, cardamom pods, star anise, cloves and cinnamon stick and cook until the onion is soft and translucent. Add the spice paste and cook gently, stirring occasionally 10 to 15 minutes until fragrant and the oil starts to rise to the surface. Stir in the tomatoes and cook 5 minutes longer.

4 Add the lime juice and generous ⅓ cup water and bring to a boil. Reduce the heat to low and simmer 15 minutes. Stir in the tomato paste, ketchup, soy sauce and sugar, and season with salt.

5 Add the fried chicken pieces to the pan and stir with a wooden spoon until they are well coated with the sauce. Increase the heat to high and bring to a boil, then reduce the heat to medium-low, cover and cook, stirring occasionally, for 40 minutes, or until the chicken is cooked through and the sauce has thickened. Serve warm with boiled rice, if liked.

nyonya fried chicken

This is a fantastic, easy-to-make dish. If you can, marinate the chicken overnight so you get to enjoy the full impact of the flavor and extra-tender chicken. The Worcestershire sauce used in the dipping sauce is an example of the British colonial influence still found in Malaysian cuisine.

SERVES 4–6
PREPARATION TIME 30 minutes, plus minimum 4 hours 30 minutes marinating and resting time
COOKING TIME 20 minutes

5 shallots, roughly chopped
1 tablespoon ground coriander
1 teaspoon ground cumin
1 teaspoon turmeric
1 egg yolk
1 tablespoon cornstarch
2 teaspoons honey
1¼ teaspoons sea salt
¾-inch piece of ginger-root, peeled and finely grated, pulp discarded, reserving the juice
2 pounds 4 ounces chicken drumsticks, fat trimmed
2 cups sunflower oil, for deep-frying
freshly ground black pepper

DIPPING SAUCE
1 tablespoon Worcestershire sauce
1 tablespoon sugar
1 tablespoon light soy sauce
1 red bird's eye chili, seeded and finely sliced
juice of 1 lime

TO SERVE
1 recipe quantity Boiled Long-Grain Rice (*see page 214*)

1 Put the shallots in a mortar or a food processor and pound with a pestle or blend to a smooth paste. Transfer to a large bowl and add the coriander, cumin, turmeric, egg yolk, cornstarch, honey, sea salt and ginger juice. Season with pepper and stir to combine. Tip in the chicken drumsticks and toss until each piece of chicken is well coated in the marinade. Cover with plastic wrap and leave to marinate in the refrigerator at least 4 hours or, for an even better flavor, overnight.

2 Remove the chicken from the refrigerator and leave to stand at room temperature about 30 minutes before deep-frying. Meanwhile, in a small bowl, mix together the dipping sauce ingredients. Set aside.

3 Heat the oil in a deep, heavy-bottomed saucepan to 350°F, or until a small piece of bread dropped into the oil turns brown in 15 seconds. Gently slide half the drumsticks into the oil and fry 10 minutes, or until the the meat is cooked through and the skin is crisp. Remove the drumsticks with long-handled tongs and drain on paper towels or a wire rack, keeping them warm. Make sure the oil is still hot, then repeat with the remaining drumsticks. Alternatively, bake the drumsticks in a preheated oven, 400°F 20 minutes, or until cooked through. Serve hot with boiled rice, with the dipping sauce on the side.

pork & mushroom noodles

There are many ways of serving noodles, but the two most common are either in a soup or tossed in a sauce (with a soup served on the side.) The latter is referred to as dry noodles and here is a great example. This dish is of southern Chinese origin, and is popular in both Malaysia and Singapore. Over time it has evolved, and one of the changes is serving it with Sambal, a chili-based sauce.

SERVES 4
PREPARATION TIME 20 minutes, plus 25 minutes soaking time
COOKING TIME 15 minutes, plus cooking the noodles

1 tablespoon sunflower oil
2 garlic cloves, finely chopped
1¼ ounces dried mushrooms, such as shiitake, porcini or Chinese mushrooms, soaked, drained and roughly chopped, and liquid reserved (*see page 217*)
12 ounces ground pork
5½ ounces bean sprouts or mixed sprouting beans
10½ ounces cooked dried egg noodles (*see page 215*)
freshly ground black pepper
2 scallions, sliced into thin strips lengthwise, to serve

SAUCE
3 teaspoons honey
5 tablespoons light soy sauce
2 tablespoons dark soy sauce
1 tablespoon sesame oil
4½ teaspoons balsamic vinegar

TO SERVE
Sambal (*see page 213—optional*)

1 To make the sauce, combine all the ingredients with 2 tablespoons warm water in a small bowl. Season with pepper and set aside.

2 Heat the sunflower oil in a skillet over medium-high heat. Add the garlic and stir-fry 1 to 2 minutes, or until fragrant. Add the mushrooms and stir-fry 1 minute. Tip in the ground pork and break up any lumps. Add 5 tablespoons of the mushroom liquid and season with pepper. Cook, stirring occasionally, 5 to 7 minutes until the pork is cooked through. Remove from the heat and keep warm.

3 Bring a saucepan of water to a boil and blanch the bean sprouts about 20 seconds. Divide the warm, cooked noodles into four serving dishes, then top with the blanched bean sprouts. Spoon the sauce over the noodles and bean sprouts, then spoon the pork and mushroom mixture on top. Sprinkle with the scallions and add 1 heaped teaspoon of Sambal to each bowl, if using, and serve immediately.

Braised Pork Ribs

This is a dish that I will always remember eating as a child. My mom still makes it often, and always with more chili than is normal to give the sauce a bigger kick. Barbecuing is a popular way to cook spare ribs, but another way, which I think is much better and I use here, is braising by slowly cooking the ribs in a broth until the meat is so tender it almost falls off the bones.

SERVES 4
PREPARATION TIME 15 minutes
COOKING TIME 2 hours
  15 minutes

1 pound 12 ounces pork ribs,
  cut lengthwise into 1½-inch
  pieces
1 tablespoon sunflower oil
4 garlic cloves, finely chopped
2 red chilies, seeded and sliced
½-inch piece of ginger-root,
  peeled and finely chopped
3 tablespoons Chinese
  fermented soybean paste
1 tablespoon Shaoxing rice
  wine
1 tablespoon dark soy sauce
1 tablespoon lime juice or
  ½ recipe quantity Tamarind
  Water (*see page 217*)
1 teaspoon honey
1 scallion, thinly sliced
  diagonally, to serve

TO SERVE
14 ounces cooked rice noodles
  (*see page 215*)

1 Bring a large saucepan of water to a boil, then carefully tip in the pork ribs and poach 1 to 2 minutes until sealed. Drain the ribs into a colander, rinse the ribs under cold running water to stop the cooking process, and set aside.

2 Heat the oil in a large saucepan over medium-high heat. Add the garlic, chilies and ginger, and stir-fry 2 to 3 minutes until fragrant but not colored. Add the pork ribs and push around the pan until well coated with the spices. Add the soybean paste, rice wine, soy sauce, lime juice and honey, and stir thoroughly.

3 Add 1 cup water to the pan and bring to a boil. Reduce the heat to low and simmer, covered, 2 hours, or until the meat is very tender and almost falls apart. Sprinkle with the scallions and serve immediately.

beef rendang

Beef Rendang is one of those quintessential curries where the extra effort of making the spice paste from scratch is unquestionably worthwhile. A Rendang can be made with lamb or chicken, but the rich and thick sauce goes especially well with beef.

SERVES 4 to 6
PREPARATION TIME 30 minutes
COOKING TIME about 2 hours
  45 minutes

2 ounces freshly grated
  coconut (*see page 216*) or
  scant ½ cup dry unsweetened
  shredded coconut
3 tablespoons sunflower oil
1 recipe quantity Rendang
  Spice Paste (*see page 209*)
2 pounds 4 ounces chuck
  steak, fat trimmed, cut into
  bite-size pieces
2 tablespoons lime juice or
  1 recipe quantity Tamarind
  Water (*see page 217*)
2 crushed lemongrass stalks,
  outer leaves discarded and
  ends trimmed
5 fresh lime leaves, bruised
2 tablespoons grated jaggery or
  soft light brown sugar
1¾ cups coconut milk
sea salt

TO SERVE
1 recipe quantity Boiled
  Long-Grain Rice (*see page
  214*)

1 Heat a skillet over medium heat and dry-fry the coconut 3 to 5 minutes until light golden brown, stirring occasionally. Set aside.

2 Heat the oil in a large flameproof Dutch oven or a wok over medium-high heat. Add the spice paste and cook gently, stirring occasionally, 10 to 15 minutes until fragrant and the oil starts to rise to the surface. Tip the beef into the pan, stir until well coated, then cook 5 to 10 minutes until sealed and beginning to brown.

3 Add the lime juice, lemongrass, fresh lime leaves, sugar and coconut milk, and season with salt. Bring to a boil, then reduce the heat to low and simmer, uncovered, 2 to 2½ hours until tender and the meat is falling apart. During the last 45 minutes of cooking stir more frequently. When the liquid starts to thicken, add the toasted coconut and mix well. Serve immediately with boiled rice.

penang assam laksa

The native name for this dish is Assam Laksa, and it is just one of the many variations of Laksa. You can use lime zest or tamarind peel (known as asam gelugor or asam keping) to add an extra level of sourness to the broth. The combination of salty, sour and spicy flavors is a bold feature that makes Assam Laksa stand out from other variations.

SERVES 4 to 6
PREPARATION TIME 1 hour
COOKING TIME 45 minutes, plus cooking the noodles

1 pound 9 ounces whole mackerels or herrings, gutted, scaled and trimmed
2 stalks Vietnamese cilantro
4 or 5 strips lime zest or tamarind peel
1 recipe quantity Assam Laksa Spice Paste (*see page 206*)
1 tablespoon sugar
4 tablespoons lime juice or 2 tablespoons lime juice and 1 recipe quantity Tamarind Water (*see page 217*)
1 pound 2 ounces cooked thick rice noodles, such as lai fun (*see page 215*)
sea salt

TOPPINGS
1 small cucumber, halved lengthwise, seeded and cut into matchsticks
2 wedges fresh pineapple, peeled and cut into strips
½ red onion, thinly sliced
1 handful of mint leaves
2 or 3 green bird's-eye chilies, seeded and finely sliced

TO SERVE
1 lime, cut into wedges

1 Rinse the fish inside and out under cold running water and pat dry with paper towels. Pour 2 quarts water into a very large saucepan over high heat and bring to a boil. Add the fish and boil a few seconds, then reduce the heat to low and cook 10 minutes. Remove the fish from the simmering stock and set aside to cool.

2 Put the Vietnamese cilantro and lime zest into a spice bag or secure in a piece of cheesecloth and add to the fish stock along with the spice paste, sugar and lime juice. Season with salt and simmer 25 minutes.

3 Meanwhile, using a fork, flake the fish, removing the bones and skin. Ten minutes before the end of making the stock, add the fish.

4 When ready to serve, drain the warm, cooked rice noodles and divide them into deep soup bowls. Lift the spice bag out of the stock and discard it. Ladle the stock and fish onto the noodles, then sprinkle with the toppings before serving warm with lime wedges on the side.

singaporean FISH BALL noodle soup

SERVES 4 to 6
PREPARATION TIME 50 minutes,
  plus making the stock
COOKING TIME 15 minutes

1 pound 12 ounces skinless,
  boneless white fish fillets
¼ teaspoon sea salt
4½ teaspoons cornstarch
4 tablespoons sunflower oil
6 garlic cloves, finely chopped
5½ ounces bean sprouts
12 ounces cooked ⅛-in or ¼-in
  rice sticks (*see page 215*)
1 recipe quantity Chicken
  Stock (*see page 210*)
2 scallions, finely chopped
sea salt and freshly ground
  black pepper

DIPPING SAUCE
1 red chili, seeded and sliced
1 teaspoon lime juice
2 tablespoons light soy sauce

1 Cut the fish fillets into chunky pieces, then transfer to a food processor. Blend to a rough paste and then place in a large bowl. In another bowl, mix together the salt, cornstarch and 3 tablespoons cold water, then slowly stir into the fish paste and mix until well combined. Season with pepper.

2 Prepare a small bowl of water and add a pinch of salt. Moisten one hand in the salted water to stop the fish paste from sticking, gather up the fish paste and shape into a ball. Pick up the ball, then slam it down into the bowl a few times until the mixture is glossy and the texture is smooth and springy. Remoisten your hand as necessary.

3 Use a teaspoon to scoop up the fish paste and shape into a ball. It doesn't have to be perfectly round. Place the ball on a plate and continue until all the fish paste has been used. Cover the fish balls with plastic wrap and set aside. Meanwhile, to make the dipping sauce, mix together all the ingredients in a small bowl.

4 Heat the oil in a skillet over medium heat. Add the garlic and stir-fry 1 to 2 minutes until fragrant and starting to brown. Remove the pan from the heat and set aside.

5 Bring a saucepan of water to a boil and blanch the bean sprouts about 20 seconds. Divide the warm, cooked rice sticks into deep soup bowls, then top with the blanched bean sprouts.

6 Pour the chicken stock into a saucepan over medium-high heat and bring to a boil. Add the fish balls, reduce the heat to low and cook in the simmering stock 3 to 4 minutes until they float to the surface. Using a slotted spoon, remove the fish balls from the stock and divide into the bowls of noodles and bean sprouts. Sprinkle with the scallions and fried garlic, and drizzle with some garlic oil. Bring the chicken stock to a vigorous boil, then ladle it onto the noodles. Serve immediately with the dipping sauce on the side.

drunken shrimp

The name itself gives a not-so-subtle hint that the shrimp are cooked in a generous amount of alcohol. Chinese rice wine, Shaoxing, is widely used in Malay cooking because it enhances the flavor and imparts a very light, earthy fragrance.

SERVES 4
PREPARATION TIME 20 minutes, plus 1 hour 10 minutes marinating and resting time
COOKING TIME 10 to 15 minutes

1 pound 2 ounces raw, unpeeled jumbo shrimp
3 tablespoons Shaoxing rice wine
2 tablespoons light soy sauce
2 scallions, cut into 2-inch pieces and thinly sliced lengthwise
1-inch piece of ginger-root, peeled and thinly sliced
1 egg, beaten
freshly ground black pepper

TO SERVE
1 recipe quantity Boiled Long-Grain Rice (*see page 214*)

1 Using a pair of poultry shears, trim off each shrimp the feelers, rostrum, legs and the sharp end of the tail. Make a slit along the back of the shrimp with a sharp knife and pull out the black vein with the tip of the knife or your fingers. Rinse the shrimp under cold running water and pat dry with paper towels.

2 Arrange the shrimp on a heatproof dish that will fit inside a wok or an electric steamer, if using. Pour over the rice wine and soy sauce, and season with pepper. Cover with plastic wrap and leave to marinate in the refrigerator 1 hour. Remove from the refrigerator and leave to stand at room temperature about 10 minutes before cooking.

3 Place a round steamer rack with legs at least 1 inch tall inside a wok. Leaving a minimum gap of ½ inch below the steamer, add water to the wok and bring to a boil over medium-high heat. Sprinkle the shrimp with the scallions and ginger, then set the dish on the rack and cover the wok. Steam 10 to 15 minutes until the shrimp turn pink and are cooked through. Keep an eye on the level of the water, adding more boiling water if necessary.

4 Two minutes before the end of cooking, pour the beaten egg onto the shrimp. Serve warm with boiled rice.

malaysian shrimp fritters & tofu with butternut squash sauce

This Malaysian salad features an interesting combination of ingredients from different ethnic backgrounds. Shrimp fritters, known as Cucur Udang in Malay, are a truly authentic Malaysian food. The spices used are typical of those used in Indian cuisine and the tofu comes from Chinese cuisine. Together, the different flavors and textures work to make a wonderfully tasty fusion dish.

SERVES 4 to 6
PREPARATION TIME
45 minutes to 1 hour
COOKING TIME 1 hour
30 minutes

5½ ounces firm tofu, cut into
  bite-size cubes
7 ounces mixed sprouting
  beans or bean sprouts
1 small cucumber, quartered
  lengthwise, seeded and cut
  into matchsticks
7 ounces Jerusalem artichokes,
  water chestnuts or jicama,
  peeled and cut into
  matchsticks
3 hard-boiled eggs, halved

BUTTERNUT SQUASH SAUCE
7 ounces butternut squash,
  peeled and cut into bite-size
  pieces
scant ⅔ cup unsalted
  macadamia nuts
4 shallots, roughly chopped
2 red chilies, seeded and
  roughly chopped
2 tablespoons sunflower oil
3 tablespoons grated jaggery
  or soft light brown sugar
1½ teaspoons sea salt
1 tablespoon lime juice or
  ½ recipe quantity Tamarind
  Water (*see page 217*)

1 To make the butternut squash sauce, put the butternut squash in a saucepan of boiling water and cook 10 minutes, or until tender. Drain, mash until very smooth, and set aside.

2 Meanwhile, heat a skillet over medium-high heat, then add the macadamia nuts and dry-roast until fragrant and starting to brown. Remove from the heat and roughly grind in a food processor or blender until you have a fine powder but still with some chunks.

3 Put the shallots and chilies in a food processor or blender and blend to a smooth paste. Heat the oil in a saucepan over medium-high heat. Add the chili paste and cook 10 minutes, or until fragrant, stirring occasionally.

4 Stir the mashed butternut squash, sugar and salt into the paste, then add the lime juice and ¾ cup water. Bring to a boil, then reduce the heat to low and simmer 5 to 10 minutes until the sauce starts to thicken, stirring occasionally. Add the ground macadamia nuts and cook 2 to 3 minutes longer. Set aside and keep warm.

5 To make the batter for the shrimp fritters, mix together the flour, turmeric and chili powder in a large mixing bowl. Season with salt and pepper, then gradually stir in scant ½ cup water to form a smooth, thick batter. Add the egg, shrimp, scallions and shallots, and set aside.

6 Heat the oil in a deep, heavy-bottomed saucepan to 350°F, or until a small piece of bread dropped into the oil turns brown in 15 seconds. Gently drop 2 heaped tablespoons of the batter into the oil and fry 3 to 4 minutes until golden brown. You can fry several fritters at a time, as long as they are well spaced. Using a slotted spoon, remove the fritters from the oil and drain on paper towels. Repeat until all the batter is used, then slice the fritters into chunks and keep warm.

SHRIMP FRITTERS

scant ⅔ cup self-rising flour
½ teaspoon turmeric
¼ teaspoon chili powder
1 egg, beaten
9 ounces raw, peeled jumbo
  shrimp, deveined
  (*see page 216*)
2 scallions, finely chopped
3 shallots, thinly sliced
2 cups sunflower oil, for
  deep-frying
sea salt and freshly ground
  black pepper

7 Bring the oil back to a temperature of 350°F. Working in batches
  deep-fry the tofu 3 to 4 minutes until golden brown and crisp. Using
  a slotted spoon, remove the tofu from the oil and drain on paper
  towels, keeping the cooked tofu warm until all of it has been cooked.

8 Meanwhile, bring a small saucepan of water to a boil. Blanch the
  mixed sprouting beans or bean sprouts 20 seconds and drain.

9 Divide the cucumber, Jerusalem artichokes, mixed sprouts,
  hard-boiled eggs, tofu and shrimp fritters onto plates. Ladle
  over the warm butternut squash sauce and serve immediately.

singaporean chili crab

This slightly sweet, hot and spicy dish is undoubtedly one of the most popular ways to prepare crab in Singapore. Fresh, meaty crabs are essential so, when choosing a crab, gently press on the underbelly. If it is firm, the crab will be more meaty. If using crab claws and not whole crabs, make sure that you crack the shell slightly before cooking, so the flesh soaks up all the sauce and the shells will peel away more easily.

SERVES 4
PREPARATION TIME 45 minutes
COOKING TIME 20 to 25 minutes

3 pound 5 ounces live brown
  or blue swimmer crabs, or
  crab claws, scrubbed
3 tablespoons sunflower oil
1 recipe quantity Chili Crab
  Spice Paste (*see page 206*)
2 tablespoons tomato ketchup
2 tablespoons chili sauce
2 tablespoons honey
3 tablespoons light soy sauce

TO SERVE
1 recipe quantity Boiled
  Long-Grain Rice (*see page
  214*)

1 To prepare each crab, pull off the triangular bony tail flap and discard. Press your thumb under the rear end of the crab and lift the body away from the back shell. Discard the shell and remove and discard the stomach bag and the gills at the sides of the body. Rinse the crab flesh and claws under cold running water and pat dry with paper towels. Pull the 2 front claws from the body and then, using the back of a knife or a mallet, slightly crack the shell of each claw. Cut the crabs into quarters with a large-bladed knife. If using crab claws only, rinse under cold running water and crack the claws slighty using a large-bladed knife.

2 Heat the oil in a wok or large skillet over high heat. Add the spice paste and cook gently, stirring occasionally, 10 to 15 minutes until fragrant and the oil starts to rise to the surface.

3 Meanwhile, combine the ketchup, chili sauce, honey and soy sauce in a small bowl. Add the sauce mixture to the wok or pan, then pour in scant ½ cup water and bring to a boil.

4 Tip in the crab pieces and push around the wok or pan until well coated with the sauce. Cover, reduce the heat to low and simmer 8 to 10 minutes until the crab pieces turn bright orange and are cooked through. Serve immediately with boiled rice.

malaysian coconut & lemongrass–scented rice with squid sambal

SERVES 4 to 6
PREPARATION TIME 1 hour, plus soaking and resting time
COOKING TIME 1 hour 15 minutes

1¾ cups long-grain rice, washed and rested (*see page 214*)
1 star anise
2 crushed lemongrass stalks, outer leaves discarded and ends trimmed
3 pandan leaves, tied into a knot (optional)
¾-inch piece of ginger-root, peeled and finely chopped
generous ⅓ cup coconut milk
½ teaspoon sea salt
4 or 6 banana leaves (optional)

SQUID SAMBAL
4 tablespoons sunflower oil
2 red onions, sliced into rings
1 recipe quantity Squid Spice Paste (*see page 209*)
1 pound 12 ounces squid, cut into rings (*see page 216*)
1 tablespoon sugar
2 tablespoons lime juice or 1 recipe quantity Tamarind Water (*see page 217*)
sea salt

TO SERVE
scant ⅔ cup raw skinless peanuts
1 teaspoon sugar
2 hard-boiled eggs, quartered
1 small cucumber, halved lengthwise, seeded and cut into chunks
2¾ ounces toasted dried anchovies (*see page 217*)

1 To make the Squid Sambal, heat the oil in a skillet over medium-high heat, then add the onions and cook until soft and translucent. Add the spice paste and cook gently, stirring occasionally, 10 to 15 minutes until fragrant and the oil starts to rise to the surface. Tip in the squid, stir until well coated and cook about 5 minutes. Add the sugar and season with salt, then add the lime juice and stir to combine. Bring to a boil, then reduce the heat to low and simmer, covered, 45 minutes, or until the sauce thickens and turns a dark reddish brown. Set aside and keep warm.

2 Meanwhile, put the rice, star anise, lemongrass, pandan leaves, if using, ginger, coconut milk and salt in a large saucepan and pour in scant 1¼ cups water. Put the pan over high heat and bring to a boil about 20 seconds. Stir with a wooden spoon to prevent the rice from sticking to the bottom of the pan, reduce the heat to low, cover and simmer gently 20 minutes.

3 Remove the pan from the heat, keeping the lid tightly closed, and set aside to steam 10 to 15 minutes until cooked. Fluff the rice with a fork and discard the star anise, lemongrass and pandan leaves, if using. Set aside and keep warm.

4 While the sambal and rice are cooking, heat a skillet over medium-high heat, then add the peanuts and dry-roast until fragrant and starting to brown. Tip the peanuts onto a plate, sprinkle with the sugar and set aside to cool.

5 Serve the rice on plates or banana leaves. Ladle the Squid Sambal onto the rice and top with the eggs. Heap the cucumber, toasted anchovies and sugared peanuts to the side before serving hot.

roti canai with dhal curry

Roti Canai, also known as Roti Prata, is served at mamak stands run by the street-food sellers you find almost everywhere in Kuala Lumpur. They are normally made by flipping the dough in the air and slapping it on the work surface until it is very thin—a fantastic sight. As you might like to try this at home, I suggest you rest the dough on the work surface and stretch it out as thinly as you can without tearing it.

SERVES 4 to 6
PREPARATION TIME 1 hour, plus minimum 7 hours resting time
COOKING TIME 1 hour 40 minutes to 2 hours

1 teaspoon sea salt
1 egg
4½ teaspoons sweetened condensed milk
1 tablespoon butter, melted
4 cups all-purpose flour, plus extra for dusting
scant ¼ cup sunflower oil, plus extra for brushing and kneading

DHAL CURRY
1 tablespoon sunflower oil
3 sprigs of curry leaves, rinsed
2 dried chilies, rinsed
1 onion, roughly chopped
2 carrots, diced
1 tablespoon garam masala
½ teaspoon ground ginger
1 teaspoon turmeric
1 tablespoon tomato paste
3 tomatoes, skinned and roughly chopped (*see page 217*)
9 ounces canned lentils, drained, or scant ⅔ cup green lentils, soaked overnight
sea salt and freshly ground black pepper

1 Mix the salt together with generous ¾ cup water in a small bowl and set aside. In a separate bowl, mix together the egg, sweetened condensed milk and melted butter until well combined. Put the flour into a large mixing bowl and make a well in the center. Slowly pour in the egg mixture and combine with the flour to form a soft dough. Cover with plastic wrap and set aside at room temperature 30 minutes.

2 Unwrap the dough and turn it out onto a lightly floured surface. Knead 5 minutes, until it is smooth and elastic. Flatten the dough and split it in half. Divide each half into 4 or 5 equal portions and roll each piece into a ball. Brush the dough balls generously with oil, then place side by side in a well-oiled dish. Sprinkle with the remaining oil and cover with plastic wrap. Leave to rest at room temperature at least 6 hours, or for the best result, overnight.

3 Rub a clean work surface with some oil and generously oil your palms. Take a dough ball and flatten it, then slowly work the dough outward from around the edge to expand it, then use your fingers to slowly pull all around the edges of the dough to stretch it out. Do this carefully so as not to tear it. Continue until the dough is very thin and almost translucent. Sprinkle some oil on top and fold the edges into the center to form a square. Air will be trapped as you fold, which will help make the roti crisp and fluffy once cooked. Set aside on an oiled dish and continue until all the dough balls are used. Let rest 20 minutes.

4 Set a cast-iron grill pan, or heavy-bottomed skillet, over high heat. When hot, add a roti and cook for 5 to 6 minutes on each side until blisters and brown spots form. Remove from the pan to a clean surface and, using your hands, gently whack it a few times moving in a circle around the roti to fluff it up. Keep warm and repeat until all the dough balls are used. Meanwhile cook the dhal.

5 To make the dhal curry, heat the oil in a skillet over medium-high heat, then add the curry leaves and dried chilies, and stir-fry until fragrant. Add the onion and stir-fry 1 to 2 minutes until softened, then add the carrots and cook 4 to 5 minutes, until the carrots are tender, stirring occasionally. Add the garam masala, ginger, turmeric and tomato paste, and stir to combine.

6 Tip in the tomatoes and lentils, then pour in scant 1½ cups water. Bring to a boil about 20 seconds, season with salt and pepper and then reduce the heat to low and cover. If using canned lentils simmer 10 to 15 minutes. If using soaked lentils simmer, stirring occasionally, 30 to 45 minutes until the dhal is very soft. Serve the roti warm with the hot dhal curry.

nyonya pineapple curry

Pajeri nanas, cooked the Nyonya way, simmers in a bright red, chili-based sauce. An alternative method for making this dish is to use curry powder, but you miss out on the pure taste of fresh spices against the natural sweetness of the pineapple. Eaten with fluffy white rice, this aromatic dish, with its slight hint of spiciness and natural sweetness of the pineapple, seems like sheer indulgence.

SERVES 4
PREPARATION TIME 30 minutes
COOKING TIME 40 minutes

1 ripe pineapple
1 tablespoon sea salt
3 tablespoons sunflower oil
2 star anise
2½-inch cinnamon stick
4 cloves
3 green cardamom pods
1 recipe quantity Pajeri Nanas
   Spice Paste (*see page 208*)
1 or 2 tablespoons grated
   jaggery or soft light brown
   sugar
¼ cup dried cranberries, dried
   sour cherries, golden raisins
   or raisins
sea salt

TO SERVE
1 recipe quantity Boiled
   Long-Grain Rice (*see page
   214)*

1 Cut the crown, about ¾ inch from the end, and the base off of the pineapple, then, with the pineapple upright, carefully slice off the skin. Don't slice too deeply to remove the eyes because you will waste good flesh. To cut out the eyes, which run neatly in a spiral around the pineapple, place the pineapple on its side on a cutting board. Position a knife at an angle alongside 3 or 4 eyes. Cut a V-shape around the eyes, remove them and discard. Repeat, following the spiral, until all eyes are removed.

2 Rub the salt into the pineapple all around, then rinse under cold running water and pat dry with paper towels. (This takes away the acidity of the pineapple.) Place the pineapple back on the cutting board on its side and cut it into ½ inch slices. Then use a small round cookie cutter to remove the core from each piece. Set the rings aside and discard the cores.

3 Heat the oil in a large saucepan over medium heat. Add the star anise, cinnamon stick, cloves and cardamom pods and cook for 3 to 4 minutes until fragrant, stirring occasionally. Add the spice paste and cook gently, stirring occasionally, 10 to 15 minutes until fragrant and the oil starts to rise to the surface.

4 Add the pineapple slices and push around the pan with a wooden spoon until the pineapple is well coated with the paste. Pour in ⅔ cup water and bring to a boil about 20 seconds, then add the sugar and season with salt. Reduce the heat to low and simmer, covered, 15 minutes, until the pineapple is soft and the liquid starts to thicken.

5 Sprinkle the dried cranberries into the pan, cover and simmer 2 to 3 minutes longer. Adjust the sweetness or sourness by adding a touch of salt and sugar, as required. Serve warm with boiled rice.

CRISPY PORK ROLLS

The ingredient that makes these rolls something really special is the bean curd skin. There are two types available; one is opaque and a medium-yellow color and the other is translucent and slightly oiled. Either type of bean curd is fine to use and can be found in most Asian supermarkets. If you cannot get bean curd skin, the pork rolls are also delicious made using Chinese egg roll wrappers.

MAKES 12 rolls
PREPARATION TIME 1 hour, plus
  1 hour 20 minutes marinating,
  resting and cooling time
COOKING TIME 25 minutes

1-pound 2-ounce piece of
  pork tenderloin
2 tablespoons sesame oil
1 teaspoon five-spice powder
2 teaspoons honey
1 tablespoon light soy sauce
¼ teaspoon ground pepper
1 tablespoon sesame seeds
2 tablespoons cornstarch
8 shallots, finely sliced
1 bean curd skin, wiped with
  a damp dish towel or
  12 Chinese egg roll wrappers,
  about 6¼ x 7 inches in size
2 cups sunflower oil, for
  deep-frying

TO SERVE
mixed fresh mint, Thai basil
  and cilantro leaves (optional)

1 Place the pork on a cutting board, then trim off any fat and the silver skin by slipping the knife between the meat and the skin; slide the blade along the tenderloin and pull away the silver skin until it is all removed. Slice the pork into strips ¼ to ½ inch thick and place in a bowl.

2 Put the sesame oil, five-spice powder, honey, soy sauce, ground pepper, sesame seeds, cornstarch and shallots in the bowl with the pork, then toss until the pieces of pork are well coated. Cover with plastic wrap and leave to marinate in the refrigerator 1 hour.

3 Remove the pork from the refrigerator and leave to stand at room temperature about 10 minutes before making the rolls. Meanwhile, lay the bean curd skin, if using, on a cutting board and cut into 12 sheets measuring 6¼ x 7 inches.

4 Place 4 or 5 strips of the marinated pork horizontally along the center of a bean curd sheet or egg roll wrapper, leaving a gap of about ½ inch around the edges. Fold the bottom edge over the filling, then fold in the two sides and roll up tightly. Lightly moisten the upper edge to seal, then place on a plate, cover with a damp dish towel and repeat until all the ingredients are used.

5 Place the pork rolls on a plate and place in a bamboo or electric steamer, then steam 8 to 10 minutes until firm to the touch. Remove from the steamer and set aside about 10 minutes to cool slightly.

6 Heat the oil in a deep, heavy-bottomed saucepan to 350°F, or until a small piece of bread dropped into the oil turns brown in 15 seconds. Gently slide 4 or 5 pork rolls into the oil and fry 5 minutes, or until the pork rolls are golden brown. Drain the rolls on paper towels and keep warm while you fry the remaining pork rolls.

7 Cut the rolls into slices ¾ inch thick and serve warm with the mixed fresh herbs, if liked.

Malaysian Madeleines with coconut, lime & chocolate

Whenever the festive season is around the corner, whether it's Chinese New Year or Eid Mubarak, these little light and fluffy cakes are being baked in most households. Some resemble French Madeleines, but traditionally they are baked in molds of varied and beautiful shapes, such as flowers, fish and sea shells. Feel free to use a mini muffin pan or Madeleine mold, if you have one. I have given the recipe a little bit of a modern twist by adding dry unsweetened shredded coconut, a touch of lime and some chocolate sprinkles.

SERVES 4
PREPARATION TIME 10 minutes
COOKING TIME 30 minutes

melted butter, for greasing
4 eggs
heaping ⅓ cup superfine sugar
¼ teaspoon baking powder
heaping ¾ cup all-purpose
 flour
1 tablespoon lime juice
zest of 1 lime
3 tablespoons dry
 unsweetened shredded
 coconut
2 tablespoons chocolate
 sprinkles

1 Heat the oven to 400°F and lightly grease a Madeleine mold or mini muffin pan with melted butter.

2 Using an electric mixer or whisk, cream the eggs and sugar together in a large mixing bowl. Add the baking powder and gradually fold in the flour using a spatula.

3 Add the lime juice, lime zest, coconut and chocolate sprinkles, and gently fold through using a spatula.

4 Spoon the mixture into the prepared mold or mini muffin pan until each cup is three-quarters full. Bake about 7 to 8 minutes until golden brown. Remove from the oven and turn the madeleines out of the mold or pan onto a wire rack. Grease the mold again and repeat with the remaining batter, then let cool completely.

sago pearls with coconut & chocolate syrup

I love coconut milk with an added hint of saltiness, and this Malay dessert, of Peranakan Chinese origin, is a splendid example of how well the sweet and salty combination works. Here you also have the blend of jaggery and coconut milk, which provide big flavors in a very simple way.

SERVES 4 to 6
PREPARATION TIME 20 minutes, plus 1 hour chiling
COOKING TIME 55 minutes

1¾ cups small sago pearls
1 vanilla bean
scant 1 cup coconut milk
heaping 1 cup jaggery, grated, or soft light brown sugar
1 teaspoon unsweetened cocoa powder
sea salt

1 Bring a large saucepan of water to a boil. Add the sago pearls, reduce the heat to medium-low and cook, uncovered, 30 minutes, or until they become translucent, stirring occasionally to stop the pearls from sticking. Add more boiling water if the sago gets too sticky. Pour the sago pearls into a colander and then rinse under cold running water, lightly rubbing the sago to wash away the starch.

2 Divide the sago pearls into 4 to 6 scant ½ cup ramekins. Press down on the sago to level the surface and make the mixture compact. Cover with plastic wrap and let chill in the refrigerator 1 hour.

3 Meanwhile, split the vanilla bean in two, using a small sharp knife, and scrape the seeds into a small saucepan. Add the coconut milk, season generously with salt, and place over medium heat. Slowly bring to a boil, stirring constantly. When bubbles start to form, remove from the heat and strain through a fine strainer into a bowl. Let cool.

4 Put the sugar, cocoa powder and ⅓ cup + 1 tablespoon water into another small saucepan over medium heat. Slowly dissolve the sugar, stirring constantly, until it becomes syrupy. Set aside.

5 When the sago is set and chilled, turn the sago out onto individual serving plates. Drizzle with the cocoa sugar syrup and then the coconut milk before serving at room temperature or slightly chilled.

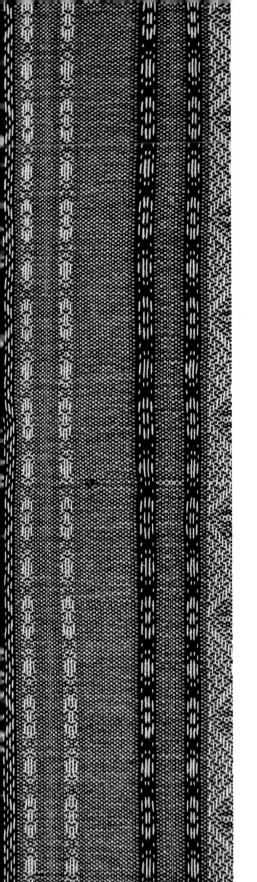

THAILAND

Thailand is a country abundant with fresh produce, dried spices and fresh aromatic herbs and roots. The Thai are a warm and smiling people who firmly believe in the way that food can bond people. They love to eat and it is because of their passion for food that there are so many amazing dishes to choose from in Thai cuisine.

Essential ingredients in Thai cooking are: fish sauce and dried shrimp, which bring pungency and saltiness to dishes (they are the main components of Nam Prik Pao (*see page 212*), a much-used flavoring); bird's-eye chilies to add spiciness; tamarind and lime bring an appetizing sourness; and fresh lemongrass, lime leaves and galangal for fragrance and flavor. Shrimp Tom Yum Soup (*see page 135*), sharp in taste with a pleasant chili kick, is an enticing dish that uses all of these ingredients in perfect harmony.

Other ingredients that are symbolic of Thai cuisine are coconut milk, cilantro roots and Thai basil. These provide the key flavors in the ubiquitous Thai Green Chicken Curry (*see page 124*). Jaggery delicately balances the sour notes in many Thai dishes, including the superbly refreshing noodle-based dishes Phuket-Style Pad Thai (*see page 132*) and Green Papaya Salad (*see page 139*).

Rice is Thailand's staple food and every meal is based around it. Cellophane or rice noodles are also very popular and are usually served in a stir-fry or a soup. Chiang Mai Curry Noodle Soup (*see page 122*) is an immediately popular example.

cHiang mai curry nooDLe soup

This curry noodle dish is from northern Thailand and takes on influences from its neighboring country, Burma. One of these is the deep-fried egg noodles, which add a crunchy texture.

SERVES 4 to 6
PREPARATION TIME 30 minutes
COOKING TIME 40 to 45 minutes

1 cup sunflower oil
1 recipe quantity Thai Red
  Curry Spice Paste
  (*see page 210*)
1 pound 12 ounces skinless,
  boneless chicken thighs, cut
  into bite-size pieces
2 cups coconut milk
3 tablespoons fish sauce
1 teaspoon grated jaggery
  or soft light brown sugar
10½ ounces dried fine egg
  noodles
7 ounces dried rice vermicelli
1 handful of cilantro leaves, to
  serve

TO SERVE
1 lime, cut into wedges

1 Heat 1 tablespoon of the oil in a large saucepan over medium-high heat. Add the spice paste and cook gently, stirring occasionally, 10 to 15 minutes until fragrant and the oil starts to rise to the surface. Add the chicken and toss until each piece is well coated in the paste, then cook, stirring occasionally, 8 to 10 minutes until the chicken starts to turn golden brown.

2 Add half the coconut milk and gently boil 5 to 7 minutes until the coconut milk starts to thicken, then add the remaining coconut milk and 4 cups water. Push the chicken around the pan until well coated with the sauce. Add the fish sauce and sugar, and cook 10 minutes longer, or until the chicken is cooked through.

3 Meanwhile, heat the remaining oil in a deep, heavy-bottomed saucepan to 325°F, or until a small piece of bread dropped into the oil turns brown in 20 seconds. Take 1¾ ounces (about one-sixth) of the egg noodles and separate the strands. Fry the strands in small batches until golden brown all around, and set aside.

4 Prepare a large bowl of ice-cold water and place it next to the stove top. Fill a large saucepan with plenty of water and bring to a boil, then add the remaining egg noodles and cook 3 to 4 minutes. Using a noodle skimmer or long-handled tongs, remove the noodles from the water and plunge a few seconds into the cold water, meanwhile bringing the water in the pan back to a boil. Return the noodles to the pan a few seconds to warm through, then drain and divide the noodles into bowls. Use the same process to cook the dried vermicelli, except cook 2 to 3 minutes.

5 Divide the chicken pieces into the bowls, then ladle over the hot curry broth. Top each bowl with the fried egg noodles and sprinkle with the cilantro. Serve immediately with lime wedges on the side.

THAI GREEN CHICKEN CURRY

My introduction to Thai Green Chicken Curry was as a teenager, and as my interest in this fresh-flavored curry grew I learned to make green curry paste from scratch. I have discovered that the most important ingredient is cilantro root because of its intense flavor. If you cannot find cilantro root, use the cilantro leaves and stalks instead.

SERVES 4
PREPARATION TIME 30 minutes
COOKING TIME 40 minutes

1 pound 2 ounces chicken
   drumsticks or skinless
   chicken thighs
2 teaspoons sunflower oil
1 recipe quantity Thai Green
   Curry Spice Paste
   (*see page 210*)
3 fresh lime leaves
1 cup thick coconut milk
3½ ounces pea eggplants
6 apple eggplants, cut in half
2 tablespoons fish sauce
handful of Thai basil leaves

TO SERVE
1 recipe quantity Boiled
   Long-Grain Rice (*see page
   214*—optional)

1 If using chicken drumsticks, rinse them under cold running water and pat dry with paper towels. Remove the skin and then, using a sharp cleaver or large chef's knife, cut each drumstick into 2 pieces through the bone. Remove the knuckles with a pair of poultry shears.

2 Heat the oil in a large saucepan over medium-high heat. Add the spice paste and cook gently, stirring occasionally, 10 to 15 minutes, or until fragrant and the oil starts to rise to the surface. Add the fresh lime leaves and chicken pieces and toss the chicken until well coated with the paste. Then cook, stirring occasionally, 5 to 6 minutes until starting to turn golden brown.

3 Add the coconut milk to the pan and bring to a boil, then add the pea and apple eggplant and fish sauce. Reduce the heat to low and simmer 20 to 25 minutes until the sauce starts to thicken, the chicken is cooked through and the eggplants are soft. Carefully scoop off any oil as it collects on the surface. Stir in the Thai basil and serve immediately with boiled rice, if liked.

THAI ROAST CHICKEN

This Thai-style roast chicken, Gai Yaang, is a very popular Thai street food. During my first visit to southern Thailand, when I was young, I remember visiting one particular market, and still remember the aromas of the Gai Yaang. Traditionally, this dish is cooked over a charcoal grill and is served with rice or Green Papaya Salad (*see page 139*).

SERVES 4
PREPARATION TIME 30 minutes, plus minimum 6 hours 30 minutes marinating and resting time
COOKING TIME 45 minutes to 1 hour

3 pounds 5 ounces chicken
1 tablespoon sea salt
1 recipe quantity Thai Roast Chicken Spice Paste (*see page 210*)
2 tablespoons fish sauce
1 tablespoon honey

TO SERVE
Green Papaya Salad (*see page 139*)

1 Remove the neck, gizzards and fat from inside the chicken. Rinse the chicken thoroughly inside and out under cold running water. Lightly rub the salt onto the skin, then rinse the chicken again and pat dry with paper towels. To spatchcock the chicken, place it breast-side down on a cutting board and then, using a pair of poultry shears, cut off the tail and cut along each side of the backbone, discarding the bone. Turn the chicken over and press down on the breast to slightly flatten the chicken.

2 Mix together the spice paste, fish sauce and honey in a large bowl, then add the chicken and thoroughly coat it in the mixture. Transfer to a plate, cover with plastic wrap and leave to marinate in the refrigerator 6 hours or, for even better flavor, overnight.

3 Remove the chicken from the refrigerator and leave to stand at room temperature 30 minutes before cooking. Heat the oven to 350°F. Put the chicken in a roasting pan. Bake 45 minutes to 1 hour until golden and cooked through. When the chicken is done the juices will run clear when the tip of a sharp knife is inserted into the thickest part of the meat. Remove from the oven and let rest 5 minutes.

4 To serve, cut the chicken in half through the breast. Take one side of the chicken and, using a sharp knife, cut through the bone to remove the thigh and drumstick whole. Cut through the joint to remove the wing, then cut the breast into 4 chunky pieces. Repeat the same steps to cut up the other half of the chicken. Serve warm with the Green Papaya Salad.

spicy chicken & pine nut stir-fry

SERVES 4
PREPARATION TIME 20 minutes
COOKING TIME 20 minutes

scant ¾ cup pine nuts
2 tablespoons sunflower oil
1 pound 2 ounces skinless
  boneless chicken breast
  halves, cut into bite-size
  pieces
1 red onion, cut into wedges
4 garlic cloves, finely chopped
4 dried chilies, seeded, soaked
  and roughly chopped
2 teaspoons Nam Prik Pao
  (*see page 212*)
2 teaspoons fish sauce
1 teaspoon honey
2 scallions, cut lengthwise into
  2-inch pieces
1 recipe quantity boiled
  Long-Grain Rice,
  to serve (*see page 214*)

1 Heat a skillet over medium-high heat, then add the pine nuts and dry-roast until fragrant and starting to brown. Set aside.

2 Add 1 tablespoon of the oil to the skillet and when the oil is hot, add the chicken pieces and stir-fry 1 to 2 minutes until sealed. Using a slotted spoon, remove the chicken from the pan, drain on paper towels and set aside.

3 Clean the pan, then heat the remaining tablespoon of oil over medium-high heat. Add the onion, garlic and dried chilies, and stir-fry 2 to 3 minutes until the onion starts to soften. Add the Nam Prik Pao and stir-fry 1 minute, then toss through the seared chicken and pine nuts. Add the fish sauce and honey, and cook, stirring occasionally, about 6 minutes, or until the chicken is golden and cooked through. Add the scallions and stir-fry 1 minute before serving immediately with boiled rice.

chilli & thai basil pork

SERVES 4
PREPARATION TIME 25 minutes
COOKING TIME 20 minutes

1 tablespoon sunflower oil
5 garlic cloves, finely chopped
1 pound 2 ounces ground pork
2 teaspoons Nam Prik Pao
  (*see page 212*)
1 teaspoon oyster sauce
2 teaspoons fish sauce
1 teaspoon grated jaggery
  or soft light brown sugar
1 handful of Thai basil leaves
1 recipe quantity boiled
  Long-Grain Rice, to serve
  (*see page 214*)

1 Heat the oil in a wok over medium-high heat. Add the garlic and stir-fry 1 to 2 minutes until fragrant. Tip in the ground pork, break up the lumps and cook, stirring occasionally, 5 minutes.

2 Stir in the Nam Prik Pao, oyster sauce, fish sauce and sugar and add a generous ⅓ cup water. Bring to a boil, then reduce the heat to medium and cook, stirring occasionally, 4 to 5 minutes until the ground pork is cooked. Add the Thai basil leaves, toss a few seconds and serve immediately with boiled rice.

THAI FRIED RICE WITH PORK & MANGO SALAD

I discovered this recipe by accident at a roadside stand run by a Malay–Thai family. This dish was one of their specialties— Thai-style fried rice topped with well-flavored ground pork and mango salad served with a small portion of Sambal. The combination of flavors is amazing, making a dish that is comfort food at its best. Mix everything together and tuck in.

SERVES 4 to 6
PREPARATION TIME 30 minutes, plus 5 to 10 minutes soaking time and cooking and chilling the rice
COOKING TIME 20 minutes

1 ounce dried shrimp
2 tablespoons sunflower oil
9 ounces ground pork
3 garlic cloves, finely chopped
1 tablespoon chopped cilantro stems and leaves
1 recipe quantity Boiled Long-Grain Rice, cooked and chilled 12 hours or overnight (*see page 214*)
1 tablespoon Nam Prik Pao (*see page 212*)
2 tablespoons fish sauce
1 tablespoon dark soy sauce
Sambal (*see page 213*), to serve

MANGO SALAD
9 ounces green mango
2 shallots, very finely chopped
2 red bird's-eye chilies, seeded and very finely chopped
2 tablespoons fish sauce
2 tablespoons lime juice
2 tablespoons grated jaggery or soft light brown sugar
1 handful of mint leaves, roughly chopped
1 handful of cilantro leaves, roughly chopped

1 Put the dried shrimp in a small bowl, cover with water and leave to soak for 5 to 10 minutes. Drain and squeeze out any excess water, pat dry with paper towels and then roughly chop and set aside.

2 Meanwhile, to make the mango salad, peel the green mango with a potato peeler, then either use a mandoline or zig-zag peeler to shred the flesh, leaving behind the flesh nearest the seed. Put the shredded mango in a bowl of cold salted water 1 to 2 minutes to draw out the acidity. Drain, pat dry with paper towels and transfer to a bowl.

3 Put the shallots and chilies in a mortar and lightly bruise them using a pestle. Alternatively, place on a cutting board and bruise with the flat side of a knife blade. Put the bruised shallots and chilies in a food processor with the fish sauce, lime juice and sugar, and blend until the sugar is dissolved. Pour the mixture over the shredded mango, add the mint and cilantro and toss to mix through. Set aside.

4 Heat 1 tablespoon of the oil in a skillet over high heat. Tip in the ground pork, break up the lumps and stir-fry 2 minutes. Stir in the garlic and cilantro and cook, stirring occasionally, 4 to 5 minutes until the pork is cooked through. Remove from the heat and keep warm.

5 Heat the remaining tablespoon of oil in a wok or skillet over high heat until smoking hot. Add the prepared shrimp and cook 1 to 2 minutes until fragrant. Tip in the cooked rice, break up any clumps and stir-fry 2 to 3 minutes. Add the Nam Prik Pao, fish sauce and soy sauce and stir to combine, and cook 4 to 5 minutes longer until heated through. Divide the fried rice onto plates and spoon the pork on top. Serve immediately with sambal and mango salad.

Beef panang curry

Rich, sweet and creamy with a dark red undertone, this is a lovely comfort dish. In comparison to the ever-famous green curry, Panang Curry (the name of this curry is derived from Penang, an island off the northwestern coast of Malaysia) gives a different dimension with the touch of roasted peanuts. Beef is the popular type of meat to use; however, pork or chicken can also work well in this recipe and are delicious.

SERVES 4
PREPARATION TIME 15 minutes
COOKING TIME 35 to 45 minutes

1-pound 2-ounce piece of beef
    fillet
1¾ cups coconut milk
1 recipe quantity Panang
    Curry Spice Paste
    (*see page 208*)
2 fresh lime leaves, thinly
    sliced
⅓ cup skinless raw peanuts
2 tablespoons fish sauce
1 tablespoon honey
Thai basil leaves, to serve

TO SERVE
1 recipe quantity Boiled
    Long-Grain Rice
    (*see page 214*)

1 Put the beef fillet on a cutting board and then, using a sharp knife, cut against the grain into ¼-inch slices and set aside.

2 Pour half the coconut milk into a large saucepan over medium-high heat and bring to a gentle boil. Add the spice paste and cook, stirring occasionally, 4 to 5 minutes until the paste starts to thicken. Add the remaining coconut milk and fresh lime leaves and cook, stirring occasionally, 3 to 4 minutes longer, or until fragrant and the oil starts to rise to the surface.

3 Meanwhile, heat a skillet over medium-high heat, then add the peanuts and dry-roast until fragrant and starting to brown. Remove from the heat and roughly chop.

4 Tip the beef slices into the pan and push around until well coated with the sauce. Cook 4 to 5 minutes longer, then stir in the fish sauce and honey. Reduce the heat to low and simmer, covered, for 10 to 15 minutes until the meat is tender. Five minutes before the end of cooking, stir in the roasted peanuts. Sprinkle with the Thai basil and serve immediately with boiled rice.

PHUKET-STYLE PAD THAI

Pad Thai is one of Thailand's much-loved national dishes and is sold from carts on most street corners. This Phuket-Style Pad Thai is unique because it is served on an omelet instead of mixing the shredded omelet into the noodles.

SERVES 4
PREPARATION TIME 20 minutes
COOKING TIME about
  30 minutes, plus cooking the rice
  sticks

2 tablespoons sunflower oil,
  plus extra for frying
5 eggs, beaten
⅓ cup raw, skinless peanuts
2¼ ounces firm tofu, cut into
  strips
3 garlic cloves, finely chopped
9 ounces raw, peeled jumbo
  shrimp, deveined
  (*see page 216*)
3 tablespoons fish sauce
1 tablespoon dark soy sauce
2 teaspoons Nam Prik Pao
  (*see page 212*)
2 tablespoons lime juice
2 teaspoons grated jaggery
  or soft light brown sugar
10½ ounces cooked
  ¼-inch rice sticks
  (*see page 215*)
5½ ounces cups bean sprouts
3 scallions or Chinese chives,
  cut lengthwise into 2-inch
  pieces
1 handful of cilantro leaves,
  to serve

1 Heat 1 tablespoon of the oil in an 8-inch skillet over medium heat. Pour one-quarter of the beaten eggs into the pan and swirl around to evenly coat the base. Cook 2 to 3 minutes until the surface starts to set. Using a spatula, turn the omelet over and cook on the other side 2 to 3 minutes until cooked through. Slide the omelet onto a plate, then repeat with the remaining egg to make 4 omelets, adding more oil to the pan if necessary.

2 Meanwhile, heat a skillet over medium-high heat, then add the peanuts and dry-roast until fragrant and starting to brown. Remove from the heat and roughly grind the peanuts in a food processor or blender until you have a fine powder that still has some chunks.

3 Heat the remaining 1 tablespoon of oil in a wok or large skillet over medium-high heat. Add the tofu and stir-fry 8 to 10 minutes until lightly golden brown, then add the garlic and stir-fry 1 to 2 minutes until fragrant. Tip in the shrimp and cook, stirring occasionally, 3 to 4 minutes until they turn pink and are cooked through. Meanwhile, mix the fish sauce, soy sauce, Nam Prik Pao, lime juice and sugar in a small bowl until the sugar is dissolved.

4 Drain the cooked rice sticks, refresh under cold running water and pat dry with paper towels. Add the sticks to the wok with the shrimp and toss until well combined, then pour over the sauce mixture. Push the ingredients around the pan until well combined, then add 3 or 4 tablespoons water and stir-fry 2 to 3 minutes. Toss through the bean sprouts and scallions and cook 1 minute, or until heated through.

5 Put an omelet on each dish, then divide the Pad Thai onto the omelets. Sprinkle with the roasted peanuts and cilantro and serve hot.

SHRIMP TOM YUM SOUP

Hot, sour, sweet and salty—these words sum up perfectly this irresistible bowl of Tom Yum Goong, to use its full Thai name. Its distinct flavors are the result of infusing the stock with ginger or galangal as well as fresh lemongrass and fresh lime leaves, which give a zesty hint of citrus. As an alternative, use chicken thighs or breast instead of the shrimp.

SERVES 4 to 6
PREPARATION TIME 30 minutes, plus making the stock
COOKING TIME 20 minutes

16 raw, unpeeled jumbo shrimp
½ recipe quantity Chicken Stock (*see page 210*)
3 crushed lemongrass stalks, outer leaves discarded and ends trimmed, cut into 2-inch pieces
6 fresh lime leaves, bruised
5 shallots, peeled and crushed
6 or 8 red bird's-eye chilies, whole and slightly bruised
¾-inch piece of ginger-root or galangal, peeled and sliced
7 ounces oyster mushrooms or button mushrooms
2 tablespoons Nam Prik Pao (*see page 212*)
2 tablespoons fish sauce
7 tablespoons lime juice
2 teaspoons grated jaggery or soft light brown sugar
½ teaspoon sea salt
2 tomatoes, skinned and cut into quarters (*see page 217*)
1 handful of cilantro leaves, to serve

1 Using a pair of poultry shears, trim off each shrimp the feelers, rostrum, legs and the sharp end of the tail. Make a slit along the back of the shrimp with a sharp knife and pull out the black vein with the tip of the knife or your fingers. Rinse the shrimp under cold running water and pat dry with paper towels.

2 Pour the chicken stock into a large saucepan and bring to a boil over medium-high heat. Add the lemongrass, fresh lime leaves, shallots, chillies and ginger, and cook 5 minutes, or until fragrant. Add the shrimp to the pan, cover and bring back to a boil. Reduce the heat to low and cook 5 to 7 minutes until the shrimp turn pink and are cooked through.

3 Add the mushrooms to the pan and cook 2 minutes, then stir in the Nam Prik Pao, fish sauce, lime juice, sugar and salt. The broth should taste sour, slightly salty and sweet. Add more lime juice, if liked. Tip in the tomatoes, bring back to a boil, then remove the pan from the heat.

4 Discard the lemongrass, fresh lime leaves, shallots and ginger. Sprinkle with the cilantro and serve immediately.

spicy steamed squid

SERVES 4
PREPARATION TIME 30 minutes
COOKING TIME 5 to 7 minutes

1 pound 2 ounces squid, cut
   into rings, and tentacles into
   pieces (*see page 216*)
10 cherry tomatoes, halved
1 handful of cilantro leaves

DRESSING
2 green bird's-eye chilies,
   seeded and finely chopped
1 red chili, seeded and finely
   chopped
2 tablespoons fish sauce
3 tablespoons lime juice
1 tablespoon grated jaggery
   or soft light brown sugar

1 Combine all the dressing ingredients in a bowl, stirring until the sugar has dissolved. Place the squid on a plate and set in a bamboo or electric steamer. Steam the squid 5 to 7 minutes until it starts to curl up around the edges and is cooked through.

2 Remove the squid from the steamer and let stand at room temperature 5 minutes, then transfer to a bowl. Toss through the cherry tomatoes and cilantro, then pour the dressing over. Serve at room temperature.

shrimp & water spinach stir-fry

SERVES 4
PREPARATION TIME 15 minutes
COOKING TIME 10 to 15 minutes

1 tablespoon sunflower oil
2 garlic cloves, finely chopped
7 ounces raw peeled jumbo
   shrimp, deveined
   (*see page 216*)
1 tablespoon Nam Prik Pao
   (*see page 212*)
14 ounces water spinach or
   baby spinach leaves
1 teaspoon fish sauce

1 Heat the oil in a skillet over medium-high heat, then add the garlic and cook 1 to 2 minutes until fragrant. Add the shrimp and stir-fry 5 minutes, or until they turn pink and are cooked through. Then add the Nam Prik Pao and cook for 1 minute.

2 Add the spinach, toss to combine and then cook 3 to 4 minutes if using water spinach, and 1 minute if using baby spinach, or until the spinach starts to wilt. Add the fish sauce and 3 tablespoons water, stirring until well combined. Serve immediately.

green papaya salad

This is a wonderfully simple dish with sweet, sour, spicy and slightly salty flavors. If you can't find green papaya, use a green mango, which can usually be found at Chinese supermarkets. However, green mango can be a bit sour compared to the milder flavor of green papaya, so you may have to adjust the acidity by adding more jaggery.

SERVES 4
PREPARATION TIME 45 minutes, plus 15 to 20 minutes soaking time
COOKING TIME 5 to 10 minutes

1 ounce dried shrimp
⅓ cup skinless raw peanuts
14 ounce firm green papaya or green mango
3 garlic cloves, chopped
2 red bird's-eye chilies, seeded and chopped
2¾ ounces green beans or Chinese long beans, trimmed and cut into 1½-inch pieces
4 tablespoons fish sauce
4 tablespoons lime juice
2 tablespoons grated jaggery or soft light brown sugar
12 cherry tomatoes, halved

1 Put the dried shrimps in a small bowl, cover with water and let soak 15 to 20 minutes.

2 Heat a skillet over medium-high heat, then add the peanuts and dry-roast until fragrant and starting to brown. Remove from the heat and set aside.

3 Peel the green papaya with a potato peeler, then either use a mandoline or zig-zag peeler to shred the flesh, leaving behind the flesh nearest the seed. Put the shredded papaya in a bowl of cold salted water 1 to 2 minutes to draw out the acidity and firm up the flesh. Strain off the water, pat dry with paper towels and add to a bowl.

4 Squeeze out any excess water from the dried shrimp and pat dry with paper towels. Roughly chop into chunky pieces and put in a separate bowl.

5 Put the garlic and chilies in a large bowl and bruise with a pestle or the end of a rolling pin until they are almost mashed. Add the green beans, little by little, and bruise until all the beans start splitting. Add the prepared shrimp and peanuts, and continue to pound and bruise until the shrimp and peanuts are roughly crushed and all the ingredients are well combined.

6 Mix the fish sauce, lime juice and sugar in a small bowl until the sugar is dissolved. Slowly add the sauce to the shrimp and bean mixture, blending as you pour.

7 When everything is well pounded and mixed, slowly add the shredded papaya, mixing and lightly pounding between each addition. Finally, add the cherry tomatoes, toss well and serve immediately.

STICKY COCONUT RICE WITH caramelized mango

A popular, very sweet, very tempting Thai dessert with a silky smooth texture and a great flavor. For a truly authentic dish, try to get Thai mangoes, called nam dok mai. These are ripened on the tree so are much sweeter and tastier. Here I've given this dish an added dimension by caramelizing the mangoes.

SERVES 4
PREPARATION TIME 15 minutes, plus 1 hour 40 minutes soaking and resting time
COOKING TIME 35 to 40 minutes

1½ cups glutinous rice
1½ cups coconut milk
4 tablespoons granulated sugar
¼ teaspoon fine sea salt
2 ripe mangoes
heaping ¼ cup superfine sugar

1 Put the rice in a bowl, cover with cold water and soak about 1 hour. Drain through a fine strainer and leave to stand 15 minutes. Line a bamboo or electric steamer with cheesecloth and spread the soaked rice over the cheesecloth. Steam the rice 20 minutes, or until it becomes translucent and is soft all the way through. Turn off the heat and let the rice sit in the steamer 5 minutes longer.

2 Meanwhile, pour the coconut milk into a saucepan over medium heat and slowly bring to a boil. Remove from the heat, add the sugar and salt, and stir until the sugar is dissolved. Set aside.

3 Remove the rice in the cheesecloth from the steamer and tip into a bowl. Pour scant 1¼ cups of the sugared coconut milk over the rice and mix well. Cover with plastic wrap and leave to stand for about 25 minutes to allow the rice to absorb the coconut milk.

4 Meanwhile, peel the mangos with a potato peeler. Take one mango and slice off the stem end to create a flat surface. Set the mango upright on the cutting board, hold it securely in place and use a sharp knife to slice downward from top to bottom to cut off one side. As you slice down, use the flat edge of the seed as your guide. Slice off the other side, then repeat with the second mango. Cut the mango flesh lengthwise into generous strips about ½ inch thick.

5 Mix together the superfine sugar and scant ¼ cup water in a large saucepan over medium-high heat, stirring until the sugar dissolves. Bring to a gentle boil, reduce the heat to medium and simmer, without stirring, 3 to 4 minutes until the mixture thickens and turns light brown. Reduce the heat to medium-low, add the mangoes and cook about 5 minutes.

6 Divide the sticky rice onto individual dessert plates. Top with the caramelized mango strips and pour over the remaining sugared coconut milk. Serve immediately.

CAMBODIA & VIETNAM

Fresh, sweet, sour and salty with a gentle spiciness; this sums up Cambodian cuisine, and the taste of each dish mirrors the country itself: warm, beautiful and full of character.

Cambodian food shares many similarities with that of Laos, Thailand and Vietnam, its neighbors. From a simple dish of Cambodian Beef Stir-Fry with Chili Sauce (*see page 152*), with a superb balance of citrus, saltiness and sweetness to a flavorsome bowl of Khmer Yellow Chicken Curry (*see page 146*), the dishes use many of the essential ingredients of all these cuisines, including lemongrass, lime leaves, cilantro, chilies, coconut milk, shrimp paste and galangal.

Rice noodles and rice are the two food staples of neighboring Vietnam, where the food is typically light and refreshing—perfect for the hot and humid climate. Grilled Beef Salad (*see page 163*), which is made with a slightly pungent-tasting fish sauce and a generous amount of fresh and fragrant basil and cilantro, is a perfect example of this light and flavorful cuisine. Vietnamese Chicken Noodle Soup (*see page 144*) is the national dish and it is flavored with the spices star anise, black pepper and cloves to give fragrance and subtle depth, something else that is common to many Vietnamese dishes.

Vietnamese Chicken Noodle Soup

During my recent trip to Vietnam, I went in search of a real pho (pronounced "fuh" and known as Pho Ga) experience. This soup is a truly satisfying and complete meal. Because it is simmered at a very low heat, with the surface barely moving, the stock is beautifully clear with no cloudiness. The gentle simmering also means the spices slowly infuse the stock, producing a rich and deep flavor.

SERVES 4 to 6
PREPARATION TIME 10 minutes
COOKING TIME 2 hours
   15 minutes

4 pounds 8 ounces chicken
1 teaspoon sea salt
½ teaspoon black peppercorns
2 star anise
3 cloves
2 whole onions and 1 onion,
   finely sliced
3¼-inch piece of ginger-root,
   peeled and finely chopped
4 garlic cloves, unpeeled
3 tablespoons fish sauce
1 tablespoon sugar
5½ ounces bean sprouts
9 ounces cooked ⅛-inch
   or ¼-inch rice sticks
   (*see page 215*)

TO SERVE
10 sprigs Thai basil
1 small handful of tarragon
   leaves, roughly chopped
1 small handful of cilantro
   leaves
2 red chilies, sliced
1 lime, cut into wedges

1 Rinse the chicken thoroughly inside and out under cold running water. Lightly rub the salt onto the skin, then rinse the chicken again and pat dry inside and out with paper towels. Put the chicken, breast-side down, in a very large saucepan or flameproof Dutch oven. Put the peppercorns, star anise and cloves in a spice bag or secure in a piece of cheesecloth and tuck it in next to the chicken.

2 In a skillet over medium-high heat, dry-fry the 2 whole onions, ginger and garlic until slightly charred, then add to the saucepan with the chicken.

3 Pour 3 quarts cold water over the chicken and bring to a boil. Reduce the heat to low and simmer, covered, about 1 hour, skimming off any scum from the surface as required. After 25 minutes, using long-handled tongs, turn the chicken breast-side up and continue to simmer until the end of the cooking time. The chicken is done when the juices run clear when the tip of a sharp knife is inserted into the thickest part of the meat.

4 Remove the chicken from the stock, rinse it under cold running water and let rest 10 minutes, or until cool enough to handle. Cut the meat away from the legs and remove the breast meat from the bone in 2 whole pieces. Return the bones to the stock and continue to simmer, covered, 1 hour longer. Shred or slice the meat, removing the skin and any small bones. Cover with plastic wrap to keep moist and set aside.

5 Take the stock off the heat. Scoop out all the solid ingredients with a slotted spoon. Set aside to cool and then strain over a large bowl through a strainer lined with cheesecloth. Give the saucepan a rinse and pour the stock back in. Bring to a gentle boil over medium-high heat, add the fish sauce and sugar, stirring until the sugar has dissolved, then reduce the heat to low and leave gently simmering.

6 Meanwhile, bring a saucepan of water to a boil and blanch the bean sprouts about 20 seconds. Divide the warm, cooked rice sticks into deep soup bowls, then top with the blanched bean sprouts. Top with the shredded chicken and sprinkle with the sliced onion.

7 Meanwhile, bring the stock to a vigorous boil and put the sprigs of Thai basil with the tarragon, cilantro, chilies and lime on a serving plate. Ladle the stock into the bowls and serve immediately with the accompaniments on the side.

khmer yellow chicken curry

Spice pastes, known as kroeung, are very important in Khmer cooking. They feature regularly in stir-fries, soups and stews. There are three distinct types of spice pastes—yellow, green and red—and it is the dominant spice used to make the paste that defines its color. In yellow kroeung it is turmeric; green chili gives green kroeung its color; and red chilies produce the bright red color of red kroeung.

SERVES 4
PREPARATION TIME 30 minutes
COOKING TIME 30 to 40 minutes

2 tablespoons sunflower oil
1 small onion, roughly chopped
1 recipe quantity Khmer Yellow Curry Spice Paste (*see page 208*)
1 pound 5 ounces skinless, boneless chicken thighs, cut into bite-size pieces
2 fresh lime leaves
1 carrot, cut into bite-size pieces
1¾ cups coconut milk
2 tablespoons fish sauce
1 tablespoon grated jaggery or soft light brown sugar
5½ ounces green beans, cut lengthwise into 2-inch pieces

TO SERVE
1 recipe quantity Boiled Long-Grain Rice (*see page 214*)

1 Heat the oil in a large skillet over medium-high heat. Add the onion and cook for 2 to 3 minutes until soft and translucent, stirring occasionally. Add the spice paste and cook gently, stirring occasionally, 10 to 15 minutes until fragrant and the oil starts to rise to the surface.

2 Tip in the chicken pieces and add the fresh lime leaves, then push the chicken pieces around the pan until they are well coated with the spice paste. Cook 4 to 5 minutes longer, then add the carrots and cook 2 to 3 minutes longer.

3 Pour the coconut milk into the pan and bring to a boil, then add the fish sauce and sugar, and stir until the sugar is dissolved. Tip in the sliced green beans and combine with the other ingredients. Reduce the heat to low and simmer 10 to 15 minutes until the sauce starts to thicken and the chicken is cooked through. Serve warm with boiled rice.

vietnamese-style chicken & pork pâté baguette

MAKES 4

PREPARATION TIME 1 hour, plus 2 hours 15 minutes marinating and pickling time and 24 to 36 hours resting time

COOKING TIME 45 minutes to 1 hour

4 sandwich-sized baguettes

1 small cucumber, quartered lengthwise, seeded and cut into matchsticks

chili sauce, to taste (optional)

2 small handfuls of cilantro leaves

PÂTÉ

9 ounces chicken livers

2 tablespoons butter

3 shallots, roughly chopped

3 garlic cloves, roughly chopped

½-inch piece of ginger-root, peeled and roughly chopped

9 ounces cubed pork loin

1 teaspoon five-spice powder

4½ teaspoons fish sauce

¼ teaspoon sea salt

1 egg, beaten

2 bay leaves

PICKLED CARROT & DAIKON

7 ounces carrots, grated

7 ounces daikon, grated

½ tablespoon sea salt

3 tablespoons honey

½ cup rice vinegar

1 To make the pâté, cut the chicken livers in half and trim off any fibrous tissues. Rinse under cold running water and pat dry with paper towels.

2 Melt the butter in a skillet over medium heat, then add the shallots, garlic and ginger. Cook 2 minutes, or until fragrant and softened, then transfer to a food processor. Add the cubed pork and chicken livers and blend to a rough paste.

3 Transfer the paste to a bowl, add the five-spice powder, fish sauce, salt and egg, and stir until well combined. Cover with plastic wrap and leave to marinate in the refrigerator about 2 hours.

4 To prepare the pickled vegetables, put the grated carrots and daikon in a bowl, rub in the salt and let stand 5 minutes. Squeeze out as much moisture as possible, then pat dry with paper towels. Return the vegetables to the bowl, mix in the honey and pour in the rice vinegar. Let stand at room temperature at least 1 hour.

5 Remove the marinated pork and chicken liver pâté from the fridge and spoon the mixture into a 7 x 5½-inch baking dish. Level the surface and arrange the bay leaves on top. Let stand at room temperature 15 minutes. Meanwhile, heat the oven to 350°F.

6 Cover the baking dish tightly with foil and transfer to a large roasting pan. Pour in enough boiling water to come two-thirds of the way up the baking dish, then place the roasting pan in the preheated oven and bake 45 minutes to 1 hour, or until the blade of a fine, sharp knife inserted into the center of the pâté comes out clean.

7 Remove the foil and bay leaves from the pâté. Let cool at room temperature, then cover with plastic wrap and let chill in the refrigerator 24 to 36 hours. When ready to serve, turn the pâté out onto a cutting board and cut into ½-inch slices.

8 Slice each baguette in half lengthwise, leaving one side still intact. Spread 2 generous slices of pâté over each baguette, then top with the cucumber strips, pickled carrot and daikon. Place a spoonful of chili sauce, if using, and a sprinkling of cilantro on top of the vegetables, close the baguette and serve. Any unused pickled vegetables can be kept sealed in a jar in the refrigerator up to 1 month.

PHNOM PENH NOODLE SOUP

SERVES 4 to 6
PREPARATION TIME 20 minutes,
plus making the stock and soaking
and cooking the noodles
COOKING TIME about 1 hour,
plus cooking the noodles

1 recipe quantity Pork Stock
  (*see page 211*)
1 onion
½ teaspoon coriander seeds
2 cloves
¼ teaspoon Sichuan
  peppercorns
9 ounces ground pork
1 scallion, finely chopped
1 tablespoon sunflower oil
7 ounces raw peeled jumbo
  shrimp, deveined
  (*see page 216*)
5½ ounces bean sprouts
9 ounces cooked thick rice
  noodles (*see page 215*)
2 tablespoons fish sauce
2 teaspoons sugar
sea salt and freshly ground
  black pepper
1 small handful of cilantro
  leaves, to serve
2 tablespoons Fried Shallots
  (*see page 212*), to serve

TO SERVE
1 lime, cut into wedges
extra bean sprouts

1 Pour the pork stock into a saucepan and bring to a boil over high heat. Reduce the heat to low and simmer. Meanwhile, dry-fry the whole onion in a skillet over medium-high heat until the outer layer is slightly charred all over. Add the charred onion to the simmering stock. Put the coriander seeds, cloves and Sichuan peppercorns in a spice bag or secure in a piece of cheesecloth and add to the stock. Continue to simmer, covered, 45 minutes.

2 Put the ground pork in a bowl and season with salt and pepper. Tip into a food processor and blend to a smooth paste. Put the pork back into the bowl, add the scallion and mix until well combined. Using a teaspoon, scoop up the paste and shape into walnut-size balls and arrange on a plate—they don't need to be perfectly round. Repeat until all the pork paste is used. Cover with plastic wrap and set aside.

3 Heat the oil in a large skillet over medium-high heat. Add the shrimp and stir-fry 3 to 4 minutes until they turn pink and are cooked through. Transfer to a plate and set aside.

4 Bring a saucepan of water to a boil and blanch the bean sprouts about 20 seconds. Divide the warm, cooked noodles into deep soup bowls, then top with the blanched bean sprouts.

5 Bring the stock back to a boil, then add the pork balls and cook 4 to 5 minutes until they are cooked through and float to the surface. Divide the pork balls into the bowls of noodles and add the cooked shrimp.

6 Add the fish sauce, a generous pinch of salt and the sugar to the pork stock and bring to a vigorous boil. Ladle the stock into the bowls, then sprinkle with the cilantro and fried shallots. Serve immediately with the lime wedges and extra bean sprouts on the side.

cambodian beef stir-fry with chili sauce

This dish was brought to Cambodia from Vietnam during the French colonization. The name in Vietnamese, Bo Luc Lac, literally translates as "shaking beef". This recipe is based on a delicious version I ate in Phnom Penh. I've added honey and used dark soy sauce to make it even more flavorful.

SERVES 4
PREPARATION TIME 30 minutes, plus minimum 1 hour marinating time
COOKING TIME about 10 minutes

1 pound 2 ounces bite-size pieces of beef sirloin
5 garlic cloves, finely chopped
½ teaspoon sea salt
¼ teaspoon freshly ground black pepper
¼ teaspoon cinnamon
2 teaspoons dark soy sauce
2 tablespoons sunflower oil
1 romaine lettuce, leaves roughly torn
2 tomatoes, sliced
1 small cucumber, seeded and cut into chunky slices
1 small red onion, thinly sliced
1 tablespoon fish sauce
1 tablespoon tomato ketchup
2 teaspoons honey

CHILI SAUCE
½ teaspoon sea salt
¼ teaspoon freshly ground black pepper
1 small red chili, seeded and sliced
juice of 1 lime

TO SERVE
1 recipe quantity Boiled Long-Grain Rice (*see page 214*—optional)

1 To prepare the chili sauce, mix all the ingredients in a small bowl and set aside.

2 Put the beef, garlic, salt, black pepper, cinnamon and soy sauce in a large bowl and mix well. Cover with plastic wrap and leave to marinate in the refrigerator 1 hour or, for even better flavor, overnight.

3 Heat the oil in a wok or large skillet over high heat until smoking hot. Tip in the beef and the marinade, and stir-fry 5 to 7 minutes, or until the beef is browned and the liquid has evaporated. Add the fish sauce, tomato ketchup and honey to the wok, and push the beef around until well coated. Cook 1 minute longer then spoon the beef onto the salad. Drizzle with the chili sauce and serve immediately with boiled rice, if liked.

caramelized salmon with pineapple

Sweet and salty with a touch of chili, this dish goes well with just about any fish, but it is particularly good with the buttery richness of salmon. If you want to try it with a white-fleshed fish, I suggest either haddock or monkfish. Fish steaks work better than fillets because they stay whole rather than breaking into pieces.

SERVES 4
PREPARATION TIME 45 minutes
COOKING TIME about 25 minutes

4 x 9 ounces boneless salmon
  steaks (about 1 to 1¼ inches
  thick), skins on
1 tablespoon sunflower oil
3 garlic cloves, finely chopped
1 small red chili, seeded and
  finely diced
2 tablespoons sugar
1 tablespoon honey
¼ teaspoon freshly ground
  black pepper
4 tablespoons fish sauce
2 teaspoons dark soy sauce
7 ounces pineapple, peeled,
  cored and cut into bite-size
  pieces

TO SERVE
1 recipe quantity Boiled
  Long-Grain Rice (*see page
  214*—optional)

1 For each salmon steak, using the tip of a small, sharp knife, carefully slice the skin away from the flesh from the bottom two sides of the steaks, leaving it intact on the upper halves. Fold the skinned pieces of fish into the centre of the steak to create a circular shape, then wrap the loose pieces of skin around the outside. Secure in place with butcher's string. (This is known as a fish noisette.)

2 Heat the oil in a skillet over medium-high heat. Add the garlic and chili, and stir-fry 1 to 2 minutes until fragrant. Add the sugar, honey, pepper, fish sauce and soy sauce, and stir until the sugar is dissolved. Simmer, stirring constantly, 2 minutes until the sauce starts to caramelize.

3 Add the prepared salmon steaks and pineapple to the pan and bring to a boil. Reduce the heat to medium. Cook, covered, for 10 to 12 minutes until the salmon turns opaque and is cooked through.

4 Remove the lid and carefully push the salmon and pineapple around the pan until well coated with the sauce. Remove the string from the steaks and serve immediately with the pineapple and sauce spooned over, and with boiled rice, if liked.

cha cha la vong

SERVES 4
PREPARATION TIME 25 minutes,
plus 30 minutes marinating time
COOKING TIME 15 to 20 minutes

1¼-inch piece of fresh
   turmeric, peeled and roughly
   chopped, or 2 teaspoons
   ground turmeric
½-inch piece of galangal,
   peeled and roughly chopped
½-inch piece of ginger-root,
   peeled and roughly chopped
2 garlic cloves, roughly
   chopped
2 tablespoons fish sauce
2 teaspoons sugar
a generous pinch of ground
   pepper
1 pound 4 ounces skinless
   monkfish, cod or pollack
   fillets, cut into bite-size
   pieces
6½ ounces dried rice
   vermicelli
3 tablespoons sunflower oil
1 small handful dill, trimmed
10 scallions, cut into 2½-inch
   pieces and sliced
small handful chives, cut into
   2-inch segments (optional)

TO SERVE
⅓ cup raw skinless peanuts
1 small handful of Thai basil
   leaves
1 small handful of cilantro
   leaves
2 red chilies, seeded and sliced
   (optional)
1 recipe quantity Nuoc Cham
   Dipping Sauce (*see page 213*)

1 Put the fresh turmeric, if using, galangal, ginger and garlic in a
mortar or a food processor and pound with a pestle or blend into a
smooth paste. Transfer to a large bowl, add the ground turmeric, if
using, and combine with the fish sauce, sugar and ground pepper.
Tip the fish into the bowl and toss until each piece of fish is well
coated in the paste. Cover with plastic wrap and leave to marinate at
room temperature about 30 minutes.

2 Heat a skillet over medium-high heat, then add the peanuts and
dry-roast until fragrant and starting to brown. Remove from the heat,
roughly chop and set aside.

3 Bring a saucepan of water to a boil and cook the rice vermicelli
2 to 3 minutes until softened. Drain, refresh under cold running
water, pat dry with paper towels and divide into four individual
serving bowls.

4 Heat the oil in a skillet over medium-high heat. Add the marinated
fish and fry, stirring occasionally, 6 to 7 minutes until crisp, golden
brown and cooked through. Add the dill, scallions and chives, if
using. Toss and cook a few seconds longer until wilted. Remove
from the heat and transfer to a serving dish.

5 Transfer the bowls of noodles, accompaniments and turmeric fish
to the table for everyone to assemble themselves.

curry FISH mousse

Traditionally, this Cambodian dish is served in banana leaves that are folded into a tray shape. Two leaves, cut into squares, are layered and then folded up at the edges to create corners, which are held in place with toothpicks. However, a simpler way to serve curry fish mousse is in small, heatproof bowls.

SERVES 6
PREPARATION TIME 10 minutes
COOKING TIME 20 minutes

1½ cups coconut milk
1 tablespoon grated jaggery
  or soft light brown sugar
1 tablespoon fish sauce
1 recipe quantity Curry Fish
  Mousse Spice Paste
  (*see page 207*)
2 eggs, beaten
2 fresh lime leaves, thinly
  sliced
1 pound skinless, boneless
  haddock loin, or other white
  fish fillets, cut into bite-size
  pieces
sea salt

TO SERVE
Tomato & Glass Noodle Salad
  (*see page 170*)

1 Put the coconut milk and sugar in a large bowl and stir until the sugar has dissolved. Add the fish sauce, spice paste, eggs, fresh lime leaves and a pinch of salt, and stir until combined. Tip in the fish and toss until the fish is well coated with the paste mixture.

2 Make up six banana leaf bowls (see introduction above), if liked, then fill with the coated fish—the sauce should nearly cover all the fish pieces. Alternatively, use six individual ⅔-cup ramekins or other heatproof bowls.

3 Place the ramekins in a bamboo or electric steamer and steam 20 minutes, or until the mixture has set and the fish is cooked through. It should be slightly firm to the touch. Let stand 5 minutes at room temperature before serving with Tomato & Glass Noodle Salad.

HOT & SPICY VEGETABLE STEW

This Cambodian dish is one of the simplest and tastiest clear broth stews that I have ever eaten. It is a little like the Thai version, Tom Yum. The combination of the spiciness from the chili with the meatiness of the mushrooms and baby corn make it filling and satisfying.

SERVES 4
PREPARATION TIME 30 minutes, plus making the pork stock, if using
COOKING TIME about 1 hour

4 cups vegetable stock or ½ recipe quantity Pork Stock (*see page 211*)
1 onion
2 star anise
¼ teaspoon black peppercorns
1 tablespoon sunflower oil
2 or 2½ teaspoons chili flakes, to taste
1 garlic clove, finely chopped
3½ ounces baby corn, sliced in half lengthwise
4 tomatoes, cut into wedges
3½ ounces dried mushrooms, such as shiitake, porcini or Chinese mushrooms, soaked, drained and cut into thin strips (*see page 217*)
2 ounces snow peas
1 tablespoon fish sauce
½ teaspoon sea salt
2 tablespoons lime juice
1 tablespoon grated jaggery or soft light brown sugar
1 handful of cilantro leaves, to serve

TO SERVE
12 ounces cooked rice noodles (*see page 215*)

1 Pour the stock into a saucepan and bring to a boil over high heat. Reduce the heat to low and simmer. Meanwhile, dry-fry the whole onion in a skillet over medium-high heat until the outer layer is slightly charred all over, then add the charred onion to the simmering stock. Put the star anise and peppercorns into a spice bag or secure in a piece of cheesecloth and add to the stock.

2 Heat the oil in a skillet over medium-high heat. Add the chili flakes and garlic, and stir-fry 1 to 2 minutes until fragrant, then add to the stock. Continue to simmer the stock 40 minutes. Discard the onion and the spice bag.

3 Just before serving, bring the stock to a gentle boil. Add the baby corn and tomatoes and cook 2 to 3 minutes until they start to soften. Add the mushrooms and snow peas and cook 2 to 3 minutes longer until all the vegetables are softened. Add the fish sauce, salt, lime juice and sugar, and stir until the sugar is dissolved.

4 Bring the stew to a vigorous boil a few seconds, then serve immediately with the rice noodles and cilantro sprinkled over.

grilled beef salad

I was treated to the best grilled beef salad I have ever eaten in Hanoi, Vietnam, and I have included it here. The sweet, sour and salty dressing really complements the slightly charred beef, and the star fruit adds a delicious, unusual edge. If you can't get star fruit, use a green apple. I've added pomegranate seeds and used cilantro and mint, instead of the traditional Thai basil, to give this salad a refreshing twist.

SERVES 4
PREPARATION TIME 30 minutes, plus 1 hour 25 minutes freezing and marinating time
COOKING TIME about 10 minutes

4 garlic cloves, roughly chopped
3 shallots, roughly chopped
½-inch piece of ginger-root, peeled and roughly chopped
1 red chili, seeded and roughly chopped
1-pound 2-ounce rib-eye or sirloin steak, wrapped and semifrozen 25 minutes (*see page 217*)
1 tablespoon light soy sauce
½ tablespoon grated jaggery or soft light brown sugar
1 tablespoon sunflower oil
1 star fruit
heaping ½ cup pomegranate seeds
1 small handful cilantro leaves
1 tablespoon mint leaves
2 tablespoons Fried Shallots (*see page 212*), to serve

DRESSING
4 tablespoons fish sauce
2 tablespoons sugar
3 tablespoons lime juice

1 Put the garlic, shallots, ginger and chili in a mortar or a food processor and pound with a pestle or blend to a smooth paste. Transfer to a large bowl.

2 Remove the partially frozen beef from the freezer and unwrap the plastic wrap. Using a sharp knife, cut the beef against the grain into ⅛-inch slices. Put the beef in the bowl with the ground paste, then add the soy sauce and sugar and mix until well combined. Cover with plastic wrap and leave to marinate in the refrigerator for 1 hour.

3 Meanwhile, to prepare the dressing, mix all the ingredients with 4 tablespoons water and set aside.

4 Heat the oil in a cast-iron grill pan, or heavy-bottomed skillet, over high heat. When the oil is smoking hot, add the marinated beef and cook a few seconds before turning the heat down to medium-high. Spread out the meat in the pan, laying it as flat as possible so it cooks evenly. Cook 7 to 10 minutes, turning occasionally, until the beef is browned and tender.

5 Cut the star fruit into slices ¼ inch thick and place in a salad bowl. Add the pomegranate seeds, cilantro, mint, stir-fried beef and dressing, and toss well. Sprinkle with the fried shallots and serve at room temperature.

STEAMED RICE CAKES WITH SHRIMP

There are many amazing local specialties in Hue, Vietnam, and I made sure I ate as many as I could during my visit. These steamed rice cakes, called banh beo, were my favorite, and are great eaten as an afternoon snack.

MAKES 16
PREPARATION TIME 30 minutes, plus cooling time
COOKING TIME about 30 minutes

heaping ¾ cup rice flour
5 teaspoons cornstarch
¼ teaspoon sea salt
3 tablespoons sunflower oil, plus extra for oiling
7 ounces raw peeled jumbo shrimp, deveined (*see page 216*)
2 garlic cloves, finely chopped
2 shallots, finely diced
1 or 2 teaspoons crushed pork rind
1 red chili, seeded and finely sliced

SAUCE
1 tablespoon fish sauce
2 tablespoons honey
1 red chili, seeded and sliced

1 Put the rice flour, cornstarch, salt and 1 tablespoon of the oil in a bowl. Gradually pour in scant 1½ cups water and mix well. Set aside.

2 To make the sauce, put all the ingredients in a small bowl with 4 tablespoons water and gently whisk until combined. Set aside.

3 Bring a saucepan of water, to a boil. Add the shrimp and cook 3 to 4 minutes until they turn pink and are cooked through. Drain, dry with paper towels and set aside. When they have cooled, put the shrimp in a food processor and blend briefly—make sure it still has some chunks in it.

4 Heat the remaining 2 tablespoons of oil in a skillet over medium-high heat. Tip in the chopped shrimp and stir-fry 1 minute. Add the garlic and shallots, and stir-fry 4 to 5 minutes until fragrant. Remove from the heat, cover and set aside.

5 Lightly oil 16 individual shallow dishes, such as dipping sauce dishes, either all the same size or a range of sizes, if liked. Stir the rice flour mixture until smooth, then divide into the dishes. Arrange as many dishes as will fit in a bamboo or electric steamer and steam 8 to 10 minutes until set. Set aside to cool, and repeat until all the rice cakes are cooked.

6 Serve the rice cakes either in the dishes or gently scoop them out, using a spoon, onto a serving plate. Put about 1 tablespoon of the cooked shrimp mixture on top of each rice cake and then sprinkle with the ground pork rind and chili. Just before serving, drizzle each rice cake with 1 or 2 teaspoons of the sauce.

grilled shrimp lemongrass skewers

In Vietnam these griddled shrimp skewers are usually served on their own. For a more complete and irresistible dish, here I wrap the extra-crisp skewers in lettuce leaves with herbs and bean sprouts. Another way to make this dish is to wrap the shrimp paste in dry rice paper. Because the rice paper isn't soaked, you get to enjoy the different textures of the ingredients—the crispiness of the rice paper, which is slightly softened by the Nuoc Cham Dipping Sauce, and the tender, moist chopped shrimp.

MAKES 16
PREPARATION TIME 30 minutes, plus 1 hour marinating time
COOKING TIME 30 minutes

1 pound 2 ounces raw peeled jumbo shrimp, deveined and roughly chopped (*see page 216*)
2 garlic cloves, finely chopped
1 tablespoon fish sauce
1 teaspoon grated jaggery or soft light brown sugar
1 scallion, chopped
1 tablespoon sunflower oil, plus extra for oiling
16 lemongrass stalks, outer leaves and stalk ends discarded, trimmed to 1¾-inch pieces
sea salt

TO SERVE
2¾ ounces dried rice vermicelli
1 small butterhead lettuce
6 sprigs Thai basil
1 small handful of pea shoots
2 ounces bean sprouts
1 recipe quantity Nuoc Cham Dipping Sauce (*see page 213*)

1 Put the shrimp, garlic, fish sauce, sugar and scallion in a food processor and blend to a rough paste without any solid pieces of shrimp. Transfer to a bowl and stir in the oil. Cover with plastic wrap and leave to marinate in the refrigerator 1 hour.

2 To prepare the accompaniments, bring a saucepan of water to a boil and cook the rice vermicelli 2 to 3 minutes until softened. Drain, refresh under cold running water, pat dry with paper towels and transfer to a serving plate.

3 Prepare a bowl of slightly salted water. Moisten one hand with the salted water to stop the shrimp paste from sticking and then place 2 heaping tablespoons of the shrimp paste in your palm. Use the back of the spoon to flatten the paste into a 2-inch circle, then slightly close your hand and place three-quarters of a lemongrass stalk along the center. Mold the paste around the lemongrass. Set aside and repeat until all the ingredients are used.

4 Line a bamboo or electric steamer with a piece of wax paper and arrange the shrimp skewers on the paper. Steam the skewers 5 minutes, or until the shrimp paste is almost cooked through. Remove from the heat. Let stand at room temperature 5 minutes.

5 Pour some oil into a cast-iron grill pan, or heavy-bottomed skillet, then use paper towels to grease the pan evenly and soak up any excess oil. Place the pan over medium-high heat. Working in batches of 5 or 6 skewers, grill the shrimp, turning frequently, 6 to 7 minutes until browned on all sides and cooked through. Remove from the pan and keep warm until all the skewers are cooked. Oil the pan again, as required.

6 Transfer the skewers, plate of accompaniments and Nuoc Cham Dipping Sauce to the table for everyone to make their own parcels and then dip them into the sauce. To assemble the packages, cut the shrimp off the lemongrass and into smaller pieces, and then fold up in a lettuce leaf with the herbs, bean sprouts and rice vermicelli.

vietnamese shrimp wraps

These wraps— each one neatly rolled in translucent rice paper with a hint of the orange and green colors from the ingredients inside showing through—look stunning. Each bite of these healthy finger foods reveals a mouthwatering combination of the fresh, clean flavors of the shrimp paired with the gentle tang of the Nuoc Cham Dipping Sauce.

MAKES 12
PREPARATION TIME 45 minutes
COOKING TIME 3 minutes

4¼ ounces dried rice
  vermicelli
12 x 6¼-inch round rice paper
  sheets
36 Thai basil leaves or mint
  leaves
24 cooked, peeled, jumbo
  shrimp
¾ ounces bean sprouts
12 garlic chives, cut into
  6¼-inch lengths

TO SERVE
1 recipe quantity Nuoc Cham
  Dipping Sauce (*see page 213*)

1 Bring a saucepan of water to a boil and cook the rice vermicelli for 2 to 3 minutes until softened. Drain, refresh under cold running water and pat dry with paper towels. Transfer to a bowl and roughly cut into 2½-inch pieces.

2 Lay a damp, clean dish towel on a cutting board and place a large bowl of warm water to the side. Take a sheet of rice paper and submerge it in the warm water about 10 seconds. Don't soak the rice paper for any longer than that or it will tear.

3 Set the soaked rice paper sheet flat on a dish towel. Arrange 3 basil leaves along the center of the sheet, then place 2 shrimp roughly on top of the basil leaves. Next, put a few bean sprouts on the shrimp and then a large pinch of cooked rice vermicelli. Mold the ingredients into an oblong shape. Fold the bottom of the sheet over the filling, then fold in the two sides. Add 2 garlic chives to the center, crossways, so one end of the chives sticks over the edge. Roll the wrap and chives up as tightly as possible. Put the wrap on a serving plate and cover with a damp dish towel. Repeat the process until all the ingredients are used. Serve the wraps at room temperature with Nuoc Cham Dipping Sauce on the side.

55SIDE DISHES

TOMATO & GLASS NOODLE SALAD

For a salad that is so easy to make, you will be surprised by just how satisfying and enjoyable it is to eat. The dressing is made up of punchy flavors, including underripe tomatoes, which are slightly more acidic than ripe ones and are often used in Cambodian cooking. If you can't get unripened tomatoes, cherry tomatoes are a good substitute.

SERVES 4
PREPARATION TIME 30 minutes
COOKING TIME 5 to 10 minutes

5½ ounces glass noodles, such as bean thread vermicelli
⅓ cup raw cashews
a generous pinch of chili powder
2 teaspoons honey
10½ ounces unripened tomatoes, roughly chopped, or cherry tomatoes, halved
½ red onion, finely sliced
3 ounces bean sprouts
1 handful of cilantro leaves
1 handful of Thai basil leaves or sweet basil leaves

DRESSING
1 garlic clove, finely chopped
2 red bird's-eye chilies, seeded and sliced
4 tablespoons lime juice
½ teaspoon lime zest
4 tablespoons fish sauce
2 tablespoons honey

1 To make the dressing, put all the ingredients in a small bowl and gently whisk until combined. Set aside.

2 Bring a saucepan of water to a boil and cook the glass noodles 2 to 3 minutes until softened. Drain, refresh under cold running water, pat dry with paper towels and tip into a large bowl.

3 Heat a skillet over medium-high heat, then add the cashews and dry-roast until fragrant and starting to brown. Remove from the heat, add the chili powder and honey to the pan and stir until the cashews are well coated. Set aside to cool. When the nuts are cool enough to handle, roughly chop.

4 Add the tomatoes, onion, bean sprouts, cilantro and Thai basil or sweet basil to the bowl with the prepared noodles. Pour over the dressing and toss all the ingredients together until well combined. Sprinkle with the spicy peanuts and serve at room temperature.

vietnamese sago pudding

SERVES 4
PREPARATION TIME 20 minutes,
  plus dried bean soaking and
  cooling time
COOKING TIME 45 minutes

heaping 1 cup superfine sugar
1¾ cups medium sago pearls
1 teaspoon green tea powder
3½ ounces peeled split mung
  beans, soaked at least
  4 hours or overnight
2 ounces kidney beans, soaked
  2 hours, or 2¾ ounces
  drained canned kidney beans
scant ⅔ cup coconut milk
¼ teaspoon fine sea salt
crushed ice, to serve

1 Put heaping ¾ cup of the superfine sugar and ⅓ cup water in a saucepan over medium-high heat. Bring to a boil, stirring constantly to dissolve the sugar, then reduce the heat to medium-low and gently boil 6 to 7 minutes until the mixture starts to thicken but not color. Remove from the heat and set aside.

2 Bring a large saucepan of water to a boil. Add the sago pearls, reduce the heat to medium-low and cook uncovered 30 minutes, or until they become translucent, stirring occasionally to stop the pearls from sticking. Add more boiling water if the sago gets too sticky. Pour into a colander and rinse under cold running water, lightly rubbing the sago to wash away the starch. Transfer to a bowl, sprinkle with the green tea powder and mix until well combined. Set aside to cool.

3 Meanwhile, cook the soaked and drained split mung beans and kidney beans, if using. Put the split mung beans in a saucepan, add scant ⅔ cup water and bring to a boil over high heat. Cover the pan, reduce the heat to medium and cook, stirring occasionally, 30 minutes, or until the mung beans are soft and almost falling apart. Add more water to the pan if the beans become too dry. Remove from the heat, add the remaining sugar and stir until well combined. Using a fork or potato masher, mash the beans to a fine paste and set aside to cool.

4 At the same time, bring another saucepan of water to a boil over high heat and add the soaked and drained kidney beans. Cover the pan, reduce the heat to medium and cook 15 to 20 minutes until tender. Remove from the heat, drain and set aside to cool. If using canned kidney beans drain and rinse well.

5 While the beans are cooking, put the coconut milk in a saucepan and gently warm it over medium-low heat, stirring occasionally. When bubbles start to form on the surface, remove from the heat and set aside to cool.

6 Divide the syrup into 4 glasses. Add the mung beans, then the colored sago followed by the kidney beans. Top each glass with the coconut milk, then add a large handful of crushed ice to each glass just before serving. Give everything a good stir before eating.

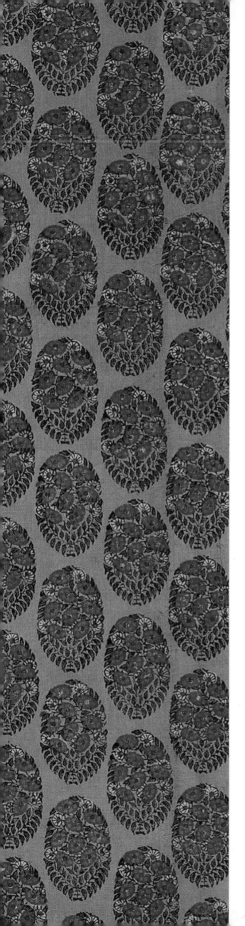

INDIA &
SRI LANKA

India is a vast country where the food varies greatly between the different regions. In the north, the cuisine is generally creamy, mildly spicy, rich and flavorsome, as in Lamb Rogan Josh (*see page 186*). In the south, dishes are often significantly more spicy and largely based on coconut, as in Fish Curry with Okra (*see page 192*) and Kerala Beef (*see page 184*). But no matter which part of India you are in, dried spices of many varieties come into play. Before the cooking starts, the spices need to be toasted and then ground, and these steps make a real difference to the taste of the final dish.

The story is similar in Sri Lanka, where dried spices, such as cardamom, cinnamon, cloves, cumin, ground fennel, pepper and turmeric are key. However, in comparison to India, fewer fresh spices—mainly just chili and curry leaves—are used. Despite this, there is a beautiful, subtle boldness and balance to Sri Lankan cuisine, and Sour Fish Curry (*see page 191*) is just one amazing example. Pandan leaves, which grow in abundance in most backyards in Sri Lanka, are one of the most important ingredients needed for cooking traditional Sri Lankan curries, such as Deviled Pork (*see page 182*). They provide a unique, flowery fragrance and flavor, but a delicious, modern twist to these dishes is to use lemongrass instead.

CHICKEN BIRYANI RICE

Biryani, a meal in itself, originates from Persia and is a highly celebrated dish in India. Don't be discouraged by the long list of spices. The time and effort you put into preparing this dish will definitely be repaid in the eating.

SERVES 4
PREPARATION TIME 30 minutes, plus about 1 hour marinating, soaking and resting time
COOKING TIME about 1 hour

1 pound 5 ounces skinless, boneless chicken thighs, cut into bite-size pieces
½ teaspoon turmeric
¼ teaspoon chili powder
2 garlic cloves, grated
2 tablespoons Greek-style yogurt
1 teaspoon sea salt
scant 2 cups basmati rice
¼ teaspoon cumin seeds
2 x 2-inch cinnamon sticks
6 green cardamom pods
2 tablespoons sunflower oil
2 black cardamom pods
4 cloves
3 or 4 dried bay leaves
1 star anise
6 or 7 black peppercorns
2 onions, sliced
2 green chilies, seeded and chopped
1 tomato, chopped
½ teaspoon tomato paste
a pinch of saffron threads
1 tablespoon butter, softened

TO SERVE
1 handful of cilantro leaves, roughly chopped
1 or 2 tablespoons dry unsweetened shredded coconut
2 tablespoons Fried Shallots (*see page 212*)

1 Put the chicken pieces in a large bowl, then add the turmeric, chili powder, garlic, yogurt and ½ teaspoon of the salt. Toss until the chicken is well coated. Cover with plastic wrap and leave to marinate in the refrigerator 45 minutes to 1 hour. Remove from the refrigerator and let stand at room temperature 15 minutes before cooking.

2 Meanwhile, put the rice in a large saucepan and pour in enough water to half fill the pan. Swirl the rice using your hand, lightly rubbing the grains, until the water becomes cloudy. Tilt the pot carefully to pour off the water. Repeat this process 3 or 4 times. The water will not be completely clear, but will be less cloudy than after the first wash. Cover the rice with water and leave to stand 30 minutes. Drain and let sit in the strainer 5 minutes.

3 Half fill a saucepan with water and bring to a boil over medium-high heat. Add the washed rice, cumin seeds, 1 cinnamon stick, 3 green cardamom pods and the remaining ½ teaspoon of salt, and boil gently 3 to 4 minutes. Drain the rice into a strainer and rinse under cold running water to stop the cooking process. Discard the cinnamon stick and cardamom pods, and set the rice aside.

4 Heat the oil in a large, heavy-bottomed skillet over medium heat. Add the remaining cinnamon stick and 3 green cardamom pods, the black cardamom pods, cloves, bay leaves, star anise and peppercorns and let sizzle a few seconds until fragrant. Add the onions and stir-fry 3 to 4 minutes until soft and translucent. Tip in the chilies, tomato and tomato paste, and stir-fry 1 to 2 minutes.

5 Add the chicken and push it around in the pan until well coated with the spices. Cook 10 to 15 minutes, stirring occasionally until the chicken is sealed and golden brown. Meanwhile, put the saffron threads in a bowl with 2 tablespoons hot water and set aside.

6 When the chicken is cooked, remove the pan from the heat and transfer the chicken and all the pan ingredients to a large plate. Now spread half the partially cooked rice evenly over the bottom of the pan that you cooked the chicken in. Drizzle the rice with 1 tablespoon of the saffron liquid, then arrange half of the chicken pieces on top of the rice. Spread the remaining rice evenly over the chicken and drizzle with the remaining saffron liquid. Then add the remaining chicken. Drizzle about 2 tablespoons water into the pan. Divide the softened butter into small lumps and scatter them evenly on top of the chicken and rice.

7 Place the pan over low heat, cover and cook 30 minutes, or until the rice is cooked and the chicken is tender. About 15 minutes into the cooking time, give the rice and chicken a quick and thorough stir. Sprinkle with the cilantro, coconut and fried shallots, and serve hot.

coorg-style chicken curry

Coorg is situated in southwestern India, an area where the cuisine is very much influenced by its geography, culture and people. In general, curries here are slightly spicier, and coconut milk is used more often than in curries from other parts of India.

SERVES 4
PREPARATION TIME 25 minutes, plus 30 minutes marinating time
COOKING TIME about 45 minutes

1 pound 2 ounces skinless, boneless chicken breast halves or thighs, fat trimmed, cut into bite-size pieces
½ teaspoon turmeric
½ teaspoon chili powder
2 tablespoons sunflower oil
½ teaspoon black mustard seeds
1 red onion, chopped
2 garlic cloves, finely chopped
1¼-inch piece of ginger-root, peeled and grated
1 recipe quantity Coorg-style Curry Spice Paste (*see page 207*)
3 tomatoes, skinned, halved, seeded and roughly chopped (*see page 217*)
2 tablespoons lime juice
scant ½ cup coconut milk
sea salt

TO SERVE
1 small handful of cilantro leaves
1 recipe quantity Boiled Long-Grain Rice (*see page 214*)
Garlic Naan (*see page 180*)

1 Put the chicken in a large bowl, then add the turmeric, chili powder and a pinch of salt. Toss until the chicken is well coated in the spices. Cover with plastic wrap and leave to marinate for 30 minutes at room temperature.

2 Heat the oil in a skillet over medium-high heat. Add the mustard seeds and sizzle 30 seconds until fragrant, then add the onion and stir-fry 2 to 3 minutes until soft and translucent. Add the garlic and ginger and stir-fry 1 minute, then add the spice paste and cook gently, stirring occasionally, 2 to 3 minutes until fragrant.

3 Tip in the marinated chicken pieces and stir-fry 5 to 7 minutes until they turn opaque. Stir in the tomatoes, then add the lime juice and a generous ⅓ cup water, and bring to a boil. Add the coconut milk, stir to combine, and then bring to a gentle boil. Reduce the heat to low and simmer, covered, 15 to 20 minutes until the sauce starts to thicken and the chicken is cooked through. Sprinkle with the cilantro and serve hot with boiled rice or Garlic Naan on the side.

tandoori chicken with garlic naan

This is one of the most popular dishes of India. The chicken is tenderized with yogurt, aromatic spices and roots, and some food coloring is added to give the chicken its characteristic bright red appearance. Here, however, I am using ground saffron to give it a slightly different color. Naan bread goes perfectly with this well-flavored chicken, so I've included a recipe for Garlic Naan. If you prefer, you could replace the garlic with fresh herbs for an herb-flavored naan.

SERVES 6
PREPARATION TIME 30 minutes, plus minimum 5 hours 30 minutes marinating and resting time
COOKING TIME about 1 hour 15 minutes

TANDOORI CHICKEN
6 chicken legs, skin removed
5 tablespoons yogurt
4 garlic cloves, grated
¾-inch piece of ginger-root, peeled and grated
2 teaspoons chili powder
1 teaspoon paprika
2 teaspoons ground cumin
2 teaspoons turmeric
1 tablespoon ground coriander
½ teaspoon freshly ground black pepper
¼ teaspoon ground saffron
½ teaspoon sea salt
juice of ½ lime
1 tablespoon sunflower oil
2 tablespoons butter, softened
1 handful of cilantro leaves, chopped, to serve
1 onion, sliced, to serve

1 Transfer the chicken legs to a cutting board and then, using a sharp knife, make 3 long, deep diagonal slits into the thigh area of the legs and 3 smaller ones in the drumsticks. Set aside.

2 Put all the remaining tandoori chicken ingredients, except the chicken and the butter, in a large bowl and mix well to make a paste. Add the chicken legs and rub the paste into the chicken until it is well coated. Cover with plastic wrap and leave to marinate in the refrigerator 5 to 6 hours or, for even better flavor, overnight.

3 To make the naan dough, stir the sugar into scant 1 cup water until dissolved. Sift the flour into a large mixing bowl and then mix in the active dry yeast granules, baking powder, salt and garlic. Make a well in the center and pour in the melted butter. Slowly pour in the water and combine with the other ingredients to form a soft dough. Add extra flour if the dough is too sticky. Turn the dough out onto a lightly floured surface and knead 10 minutes, until it is smooth and elastic. Place the dough back in the bowl, cover with a damp dish towel and let stand in a warm place 1 to 1½ hours, or until the dough has doubled in size.

4 Turn the risen dough onto a lightly floured surface and divide into 2 portions. Knead each portion 2 minutes, roll into a cylinder and divide into 5 equal pieces. Cover the dough that you are not using with a damp dish towel, then roll one piece of dough into a ball and flatten it with your hand. Using a rolling pin, roll the dough into a 5-inch disk about ¼ inch in thickness. Put the disk on a floured tray, cover with a damp dish towel and repeat for the remaining dough balls.

GARLIC NAAN
1 teaspoon sugar
scant 3 cups all-purpose flour,
 plus extra for dusting
1 teaspoon active dry yeast
 granules
1 teaspoon baking powder
¼ teaspoon fine sea salt
6 garlic cloves, finely chopped
¼ cup butter, melted, plus
 extra for greasing

TO SERVE
1 lime, cut into wedges

5 Heat a cast-iron grill pan, or heavy-bottomed skillet, over high heat and grease with a little melted butter. Add a portion of dough and cook 3 to 4 minutes on each side. When it blisters and brown spots form, add a small knob of butter to one side of the naan. When it melts, turn the naan over and repeat with another knob of butter on the other side, then transfer the naan to a cookie sheet and keep it warm until all the naan have been cooked.

6 Meanwhile, remove the marinated chicken from the refrigerator, pour off any excess liquid and let stand at room temperature 25 to 30 minutes before cooking. Heat the oven to 400°F. Place a rack in a roasting pan and arrange the chicken legs on the rack. Smear some of the butter over each chicken leg, then put in the oven 30 to 35 minutes until cooked through. The chicken is done when the juices run clear when the tip of a sharp knife is inserted into the thickest part of the meat.

7 Sprinkle with the cilantro and onion, and serve hot with the naan bread and lime wedges on the side.

Deviled Pork

This Sri Lankan dish is always a hit. Because the meat is slowly cooked in a well-flavored sauce, rich and deep aromas develop and the tender meat melts in your mouth.

SERVES 4 to 6
PREPARATION TIME 20 minutes
COOKING TIME 1 hour
   25 minutes

2 tablespoons sunflower oil
2 sprigs curry leaves
2 black cardamom pods
2 cloves
2-inch cinnamon stick
1 onion, chopped
2 green chilies, seeded and
   halved
4 garlic cloves, finely chopped
¾-inch piece of ginger-root,
   peeled and grated
1 teaspoon chili powder
1 teaspoon turmeric
½ teaspoon ground cumin
1 teaspoon ground coriander
1 pound 12 ounces boned pork
   shoulder, trimmed and cut
   into bite-size pieces
2 tomatoes, skinned and
   roughly chopped
   (*see page 217*)
3 crushed lemongrass stalks,
   outer leaves discarded and
   ends trimmed, or 3 pandan
   leaves, tied into a knot
½ teaspoon sea salt
1 tablespoon lime juice

TO SERVE
1 recipe quantity Boiled
   Long-Grain Rice
   (*see page 214*)

1 Heat the oil in a large, heavy-bottomed saucepan over medium-high heat. Add the curry leaves, cardamom pods, cloves and cinnamon stick, and let sizzle a few seconds. Then add the onion and stir-fry for 2 to 3 minutes until soft and translucent. Add the chilies, garlic and ginger, and stir-fry 1 to 2 minutes until fragrant. Add the chili powder, turmeric, cumin and coriander, and stir-fry 1 minute. Tip in the pork, tomatoes, pandan leaves or lemongrass stalks and salt, and toss until the pork is well coated with the spices.

2 Pour in the lime juice and scant 2¼ cups water, increase the heat to high and bring to a boil. Cover the pan, reduce the heat to low and simmer, 1 hour 15 minutes until the pork is tender and the sauce has thickened, stirring occasionally. Serve hot with boiled rice.

keraLa Beef

This great curry, from Kerala in southwestern India, is a terrific standby dish because it is can be thrown together quickly and then left on the stovetop to cook. The fresh coconut provides depth of flavor and also helps to thicken the sauce.

SERVES 4
PREPARATION TIME 35 minutes, plus 30 minutes marinating time
COOKING TIME about 45 minutes

1 pound 2 ounces beef fillet, cut into bite-size pieces
3 garlic cloves, finely grated
¼-inch piece of ginger-root, peeled and grated
1 teaspoon turmeric
¼ teaspoon freshly ground black pepper
2 teaspoons ground coriander
2 teaspoons ground cumin
2 teaspoons chili powder
1 tablespoon sunflower oil
1 onion, chopped
2 green bird's-eye chilies, whole
2 sprigs curry leaves
1 tomato, skinned and roughly chopped (*see page 217*)
½ ounce coconut flesh, thinly sliced (*see page 216*), or 2½ tablespoons dry unsweetened shredded coconut, plus extra to serve
sea salt

TO SERVE
1 recipe quantity Boiled Long-Grain Rice (*see page 214*)

1 Put the beef in a bowl, add the garlic, ginger, turmeric, pepper, coriander, cumin and chili powder, and toss until the beef is well coated with the spices. Season with salt, then cover with plastic wrap and leave to marinate 30 minutes at room temperature.

2 Heat the oil in a heavy-bottomed saucepan over medium-high heat. Add the onion, chilies and curry leaves and stir-fry 2 to 3 minutes until the onions are soft and translucent. Tip in the marinated beef, toss until it is well coated with all the other ingredients and cook 5 minutes, stirring occasionally.

3 Add the tomato and coconut. Pour in scant ⅔ cup water and stir well. Bring to a boil, then reduce the heat to low and simmer, stirring occasionally, 30 to 35 minutes until the beef is tender and the sauce starts to thicken. Sprinkle with extra coconut and serve warm with boiled rice.

Lamb rogan josh

Of Kashmir origin, Rogan Josh has become a highly popular dish in both India and Pakistan. It is very aromatic, but there is no secret to this dish—the meat gets its flavor from the many spices used. The yogurt helps to tenderize the meat and is the base for the creamy sauce that provides a coating.

SERVES 4
PREPARATION TIME 15 minutes, plus minimum 2 hours marinating time
COOKING TIME about 1 hour

1 pound 5 ounces boned lamb shoulder, trimmed and cut into bite-size pieces
1 teaspoon chili powder
1 teaspoon turmeric
scant ½ cup strained plain yogurt
5 green cardamom pods
½ teaspoon black peppercorns
5 or 6 cloves
1 star anise
1¼-inch cinnamon stick
3 or 4 dried bay leaves
1 tablespoon ground coriander
½ tablespoon ground cumin
1 tablespoon sunflower oil
2 onions, chopped
5 garlic cloves, finely chopped
1¼-inch piece of ginger-root, peeled and grated
1 tablespoon tomato paste
1 small handful of cilantro leaves, to serve

TO SERVE
1 lime, cut into wedges
1 recipe quantity Boiled Long-Grain Rice (*see page 214*)

1 Put the lamb in a large bowl, then add the chili powder, turmeric and yogurt, and toss until all the pieces of lamb are well coated with the marinade. Cover with plastic wrap and leave to marinate in the refrigerator 2 to 3 hours or, for an even better flavor, overnight.

2 Put the cardamom pods, peppercorns, cloves, star anise, cinnamon stick and bay leaves in a food processor or coffee grinder and grind until powdery. Transfer the spices to a bowl and add the coriander and cumin. Place a skillet over medium heat, then add the spice powder and dry-fry, stirring frequently, 2 to 3 minutes until aromatic. Set aside to cool.

3 Heat the oil in a heavy-bottomed saucepan over medium heat. Add the spice powder and let sizzle a few seconds, then add the onions and stir-fry 2 to 3 minutes until soft and translucent. Add the garlic and ginger and stir-fry 1 to 2 minutes until fragrant. Tip in the marinated lamb, push around the pan until well coated with the spices, then cook, stirring occasionally, 15 to 20 minutes until the meat is sealed and browned.

4 Add scant ⅔ cup water, bring to a boil a few seconds, skim any fat or scum off the surface and add the tomato paste. Reduce the heat to low and simmer 20 to 25 minutes until the meat is tender and almost falling apart. About 15 minutes into the cooking time, or when the pork becomes slightly dry, add anotherscant ½ cup water. Sprinkle with the cilantro and serve warm with lime wedges on the side and boiled rice.

Lamb Korma

SERVES 4
PREPARATION TIME 15 minutes,
 plus 30 minutes marinating time
COOKING TIME about 2 hours
 15 minutes

1 pound 9 ounces boned lamb
 shoulder, trimmed and cut
 into bite-size pieces
1 teaspoon turmeric
2 tablespoons sunflower oil
2-inch cinnamon stick
½ teaspoon black mustard
 seeds
2 cloves
3 green cardamom pods
2 star anise
3 or 4 black peppercorns
1 onion, roughly chopped
¾-inch piece of ginger-root,
 peeled and grated
4 garlic cloves, finely chopped
2 red chilies, seeded and
 halved lengthwise
1 teaspoon ground coriander
½ teaspoon ground cumin
2 tomatoes, skinned and
 roughly chopped
 (*see page 217*)
1 tablespoon tomato paste
scant ⅔ cup coconut milk
½ teaspoon sea salt
7 ounces butternut squash,
 peeled, seeded and cut into
 wedges
1 handful of cilantro leaves,
 chopped, to serve

TO SERVE
1 recipe quantity Boiled
 Long-Grain Rice,
 (*see page 214*)

1 Put the lamb in a large bowl, then add the turmeric and toss until
 all the pieces are well coated with the spices. Cover with plastic
 wrap and leave to marinate 30 minutes at room temperature.

2 Heat the oil in a large saucepan over medium heat. Add the
 cinnamon stick, mustard seeds, cloves, cardamom pods, star anise
 and peppercorns, and let sizzle a few seconds until fragrant, then
 add the onion and stir-fry 2 to 3 minutes until soft and translucent.
 Add the ginger, garlic and chilies and stir-fry 2 to 3 minutes until
 fragrant, then add the coriander, cumin, tomatoes and tomato paste
 and mix well. Tip in the marinated lamb, toss until the lamb is well
 coated with all the other ingredients, then cook, stirring
 occasionally, 15 to 20 minutes until the meat is sealed and browned.

3 Add the coconut milk, salt and 2 cups water to the pan, mix well and
 bring to a boil. Reduce the heat to low and simmer, uncovered, 30
 minutes, then add the butternut squash and toss until well coated
 with the sauce. Simmer 1 hour 15 minutes longer, or until the meat
 is tender. Sprinkle with the cilantro and serve hot with boiled rice.

sour FISH curry

This is a Sri Lankan specialty. An island nation, Sri Lanka is surrounded by the Indian Ocean where fish, such as tuna is abundant. Spices and fish go very well together, as the bolder touches of fragrant spices really complement the more subtle flavors of the fish.

SERVES 4
PREPARATION TIME 10 minutes
COOKING TIME 15 to 25 minutes

2 tablespoons sunflower oil
2 cloves
2 green cardamom pods
1 red onion, roughly chopped
2 sprigs curry leaves
1 recipe quantity Sour Fish
  Curry Spice Paste
  (*see page 209*)
1 tomato, skinned and roughly
  chopped (*see page 217*)
1 tablespoon lime juice or
  ½ recipe quantity Tamarind
  Water (*see page 217*)
1 tablespoon honey
1 pound 2 ounces skinless,
  boneless tuna or salmon
  steaks, cut into bite-size
  pieces
sea salt

TO SERVE
1 recipe quantity Boiled
  Long-Grain Rice
  (*see page 214*)

1 Heat the oil in a heavy-bottomed saucepan over medium-high heat. Add the cloves and cardamom pods and let sizzle a few seconds, then add the onion and curry leaves and stir-fry 2 to 3 minutes until the onion is soft and translucent. Add the spice paste and cook 5 to 7 minutes until fragrant, stirring occasionally, then add the tomato and cook 5 minutes longer.

2 Add the lime juice and scant ½ cup water and bring to a boil. Stir in the honey and tuna and season with salt, then reduce the heat to low and simmer, stirring occasionally, 5 to 10 minutes until the fish is cooked through and the liquid has started to evaporate. Serve hot with boiled rice.

FISH Curry WITH Okra

Okra, also known as lady's fingers, are a great addition to curry dishes because they go extremely well with spices. When raw, they have a crunchy texture but cooked pods turn soft and gummy inside, and really soak up the flavors of the sauce.

SERVES 4
PREPARATION TIME 20 minutes
COOKING TIME 25 minutes

2 tablespoons sunflower oil
¼ teaspoon black mustard
 seeds
3 sprigs curry leaves
1 red onion, sliced into rings
2 garlic cloves, finely chopped
½-inch piece of ginger-root,
 peeled and finely grated
1 teaspoon ground coriander
½ teaspoon ground cumin
2 teaspoons chili powder
½ teaspoon turmeric
½ teaspoon sea salt
1 teaspoon honey
1 tablespoon lime juice
2 tomatoes, skinned and
 quartered (*see page 217*)
1 cup coconut milk
3 ounces okra
2 mackerel, cleaned and gutted
 and cut into 1¼-inch slices

TO SERVE
1 recipe quantity Boiled
 Long-Grain Rice
 (*see page 214*)

1 Heat the oil in a large saucepan over medium-high heat. Add the mustard seeds and let sizzle a few seconds, then add the curry leaves and cook 1 minute, or until fragrant. Add the onion, garlic and ginger and stir-fry 2 to 3 minutes until fragrant and the onion is soft and translucent. Stir in the coriander, cumin, chili powder, turmeric, salt, honey and lime juice, then add the tomatoes and mix in well.

2 Pour the coconut milk and ¼ cup water into the pan and bring to a boil, then add the okra, reduce the heat to low, cover and simmer, stirring occasionally, 10 to 15 minutes until tender. Add the mackerel slices and cook, stirring occasionally, 5 minutes, or until the flesh turns opaque. Serve hot with boiled rice.

shrimp curry

If you love seafood you will love this Indian dish, which has mild but deep, aromatic flavors. The shrimp are cooked in their shells, adding extra sweetness to the curry sauce, whereas the coconut milk adds silkiness. If you prefer a spicy curry, replace the chili powder in the spice paste with ground, dried chilies —a guaranteed spice kick!

SERVES 4
PREPARATION TIME 30 minutes
COOKING TIME 15 to 20 minutes

1 pound 2 ounces raw,
  unpeeled jumbo shrimp
1 tablespoon sunflower oil
¼ teaspoon black mustard
  seeds
2 sprigs curry leaves
1 onion, chopped
2 garlic cloves, finely chopped
½-inch piece of ginger-root,
  peeled and finely chopped
1 teaspoon chili powder
½ teaspoon turmeric
1 teaspoon ground coriander
¼ teaspoon cinnamon
½ teaspoon ground cumin
½ teaspoon sea salt
1 teaspoon sugar
1 tablespoon lime juice
1 cup coconut milk
1 tablespoon cilantro leaves,
  to serve

TO SERVE
1 recipe quantity Boiled
  Long-Grain Rice
  (*see page 214*)

1 Heat the oil in a heavy-bottomed saucepan over medium-high heat. Add the black mustard seeds and let sizzle a few seconds, then stir in the curry leaves and cook 1 minute, or until fragrant. Add the onion, garlic and ginger and stir-fry 3 to 5 minutes until fragrant and the onion is soft and translucent.

2 Add the chili powder, turmeric, coriander, cinnamon, cumin, salt, sugar and lime juice to the pan, and stir until all the ingredients are well combined. Pour in the coconut milk and bring to a boil, then reduce the heat to low. Add the shrimp, stirring until well coated with the sauce, then cover and simmer, stirring occasionally, 5 to 10 minutes until the shrimp turn pink and are cooked through. Sprinkle the cilantro leaves on top and serve hot with boiled rice.

paneer & spinach curry

This is a hearty northern Indian dish with a rich and creamy gravy based on tomatoes and spinach and flavored with spices. The mild paneer cheese used in this recipe is fried in a skillet until the outer layers crisp, and then cooked and coated with the aromatic sauce. The result is a delicious dish that is also suitable for vegetarians.

SERVES 4
PREPARATION TIME 15 minutes
COOKING TIME 20 to 25 minutes

5½ ounces baby spinach leaves
2 tablespoons sunflower oil
9 ounces paneer cheese, cubed
2 onions, chopped
2 green chilies, seeded and
  halved lengthwise
2 garlic cloves, finely chopped
½-inch piece of ginger-root,
  peeled and grated
1 teaspoon ground coriander
1 teaspoon ground cumin
1 teaspoon turmeric
½ teaspoon chili powder
3 tomatoes, skinned and
  roughly chopped (*see
  page 217*)
sea salt

TO SERVE
1 recipe quantity Boiled
  Long-Grain Rice
  (*see page 214*)

1 Bring a saucepan of water to a boil, add the spinach and blanch for 1 minute. Drain, squeezing out as much water as possible, then transfer the spinach to a food processor and blend to a smooth paste. Set aside.

2 Heat 1 tablespoon of the oil in a skillet over medium-high heat. Add the paneer and fry, stirring frequently, 6 to 8 minutes until it has browned on all sides. Set aside.

3 Pour the remaining tablespoon of oil in a saucepan over medium-high heat. Add the onions and chilies and stir-fry 2 to 3 minutes until the onions are soft and translucent. Add the garlic and ginger and stir-fry 1 to 2 minutes until fragrant, then stir in the coriander, cumin, turmeric and chili powder. Add the tomatoes, spinach paste and scant ¼ cup water, and bring to a boil. Reduce the heat to low and simmer 10 minutes, or until the sauce is thickened, stirring occasionally. Add the paneer, stir to combine with the sauce and season with salt. Serve warm with boiled rice.

cashew & coconut curry

Cashews have a delicate flavor that complement the range of different spices in this delicious curry, and when they soften, they help create a really smooth and creamy sauce. This is a genuine classic Sri Lankan dish that is often served with other curries and is usually included on the menu for special occasions.

SERVES 4 to 6
PREPARATION TIME 15 minutes
COOKING TIME about 45 minutes

1 teaspoon ground coriander
½ teaspoon ground cumin
1 teaspoon turmeric
2 tablespoons sunflower oil
1 onion, chopped
2 crushed lemongrass stalks, outer leaves discarded and ends trimmed, or 2 pandan leaves, tied into a knot
2-inch cinnamon stick
¾-inch piece of ginger-root, peeled and grated
3 garlic cloves, finely minced
1 teaspoon chili powder
½ teaspoon freshly ground black pepper
2 cups cashews
1½ cups coconut milk
1 teaspoon sugar
1 teaspoon sea salt
1 handful of cilantro leaves, chopped, to serve
1 handful of mint leaves, chopped, to serve

TO SERVE
1 recipe quantity Boiled Long-Grain Rice
(*see page 214*)

1 Heat a heavy-bottomed skillet over medium-high heat. Add the coriander, cumin and turmeric and dry-fry 1 to 2 minutes until fragrant. Remove from the heat and set aside.

2 Place the oil in a large saucepan over medium-high heat. Add the onion and stir-fry 2 to 3 minutes until soft and translucent. Tip in the lemongrass stalks and cinnamon stick and stir-fry 1 minute, then add the ginger and garlic and stir-fry 2 minutes, or until fragrant. Stir in the toasted spice powder, chili powder and pepper, then toss through the cashews until well coated with the spices.

3 Pour in the coconut milk and scant ½ cup water. Bring to a boil, then reduce the heat to low, cover and simmer 15 minutes, stirring occasionally.

4 Add the sugar and salt, stir to mix well, then continue to simmer 15 minutes longer until the cashews start to soften. Sprinkle the cilantro and mint on top and serve hot with boiled rice.

eggplant curry

Eggplant is a great choice for curry because, when cooked, it becomes very soft and tender. It also acts like a sponge, absorbing the spicy sauce. Eggplant's unique flavor goes particularly well in this recipe. If you can get them, baby eggplant, which are slim and oblong in shape, work really well in this dish because they have a softer texture when cooked.

SERVES 4
PREPARATION TIME 15 minutes, plus 30 minutes resting time
COOKING TIME 25 minutes

9 ounces baby eggplants or
   large eggplant
2 tablespoons sunflower oil
½ teaspoon black mustard
   seeds
1 onion, chopped
1 recipe quantity Eggplant
   Curry Spice Paste
   (*see page 206*)
3½ ounces sweet potato,
   peeled and cut into cubes
1 tablespoon lime juice
sea salt

TO SERVE
Garlic Naan
   (*see page 180*)

1 Cut the baby eggplants in half lengthwise or the large eggplant in slices about ½ inch thick, then arrange in a baking pan, cut sides facing up, and sprinkle generously with salt. Let stand 30 minutes, then rinse under cold running water and pat dry with paper towels. Set aside.

2 Heat the oil in a large, deep, heavy-bottomed skillet. Add the mustard seeds and let sizzle a few seconds, then add the onion and stir-fry 2 to 3 minutes until soft and translucent. Add the spice paste and cook gently, stirring occasionally, 5 to 7 minutes until fragrant.

3 Tip the eggplants and sweet potato cubes into the pan, toss until well coated with the paste, then cook, stirring occasionally, 5 minutes, or until they start to soften. Add the lime juice and scant ¼ cup water and season with salt. Reduce the heat to low and cook, covered, 10 minutes, or until the eggplant and sweet potato are soft. Serve hot with Garlic Naan.

masaLa Dosa

My love of Indian food started when I was eight years old when my mom served me my first Roti Canai (see page 112). One of my all-time favorites is now Masala Dosa—crispy roti wrapped with masala squash and served with any kind of curry sauce and chutney you like.

MAKES about 8
PREPARATION TIME 20 minutes, plus soaking the dhal and rice overnight and 3 to 4 hours fermenting time
COOKING TIME 30 to 45 minutes

1 tablespoon sunflower oil, plus extra for oiling
½ teaspoon black mustard seeds
2 sprigs curry leaves
1 small butternut squash, seeded, peeled and diced
2 carrots, diced
½ teaspoon ground coriander
¼ teaspoon ground cumin
½ teaspoon turmeric
¼ teaspoon chili powder
sea salt and freshly ground black pepper

DOSA
½ cup split white or black urad dal, washed and soaked overnight
¾ cup basmati rice, washed and soaked overnight
¼ teaspoon chili powder

TO SERVE
Dhal Curry (*see page 114—optional*)
Sambal (*see page 213*)
yogurt

1 To make the dosa batter, drain and rinse the soaked urad dal and basmati rice under cold running water, drain again and put in a food processor or blender. Blitz a few seconds, then gradually pour in a scant 1¼ cup water until a smooth paste forms. Transfer the mixture to a bowl, add the chili powder and season with salt and pepper. Cover with plastic wrap and let stand at room temperature 3 to 4 hours to allow the batter to ferment.

2 Heat the oil in a skillet over medium-high heat. Add the mustard seeds and curry leaves and let sizzle a few seconds, then add the butternut squash and carrots and cook, stirring occasionally, 7 to 8 minutes until they start to soften. Add the coriander, cumin, turmeric and chili powder, and season with salt and pepper. Pour scant ⅔ cup water into the pan and bring to a boil. Reduce the heat to low and cook, covered, 15 to 20 minutes until the squash and carrots are softened. Set aside and keep warm.

3 Meanwhile, pour some oil into a large, nonstick skillet or crêpe pan over medium-high heat, then use a paper towel to grease the pan evenly and soak up any excess oil. When the pan is hot, ladle scant ¼ cup of the dosa batter into the pan and use the base of the ladle to spread the mixture out as evenly as possible, using a circular motion, until about 9 inches in diameter. Cook 2 to 3 minutes on each side until golden brown and crisp around the edges.

4 Transfer the dosa to a clean surface and put 2 or 3 tablespoons of the butternut squash mixture in the center and mold into an oblong shape. Fold the dosa in half over the mixture, then transfer to a serving plate and keep warm. Repeat until all the batter is used. Serve immediately with Dhal Curry, Sambal and yogurt, if liked.

Beef & Vegetable Roti Package

MAKES 14
PREPARATION TIME 30 minutes, plus 1 hour resting time
COOKING TIME about 1 hour

7 ounces sweet potatoes, peeled and diced
5½ ounces russet potatoes, peeled and diced
1 tablespoon sunflower oil, plus extra for oiling
1 onion, finely chopped
1 sprig curry leaves, finely chopped
1 teaspoon ground cumin
1 teaspoon ground coriander
½ teaspoon chili powder
¼ teaspoon turmeric
1 small carrot, cut into matchsticks
2 scallions, finely chopped
9 ounces ground beef
sea salt and freshly ground black pepper

ROTI DOUGH
½ teaspoon sea salt
2 cups all-purpose flour
1 tablespoon sunflower oil, plus extra for kneading and oiling

TO SERVE
chili sauce (optional)

1 To make the roti dough, dissolve the salt in scant ⅔ cup water. Put the flour in a large mixing bowl, make a well in the center and add the oil. Slowly pour in the salted water and combine with the other ingredients to form a soft dough. Knead 10 minutes, or until the dough is smooth and elastic, then shape into a ball. Cover with plastic wrap and let stand at room temperature about 30 minutes.

2 Bring a saucepan of well-salted water to the boil. Tip in both the sweet and russet potatoes and cook 10 to 15 minutes until soft. Drain well, then roughly mash with a fork and set aside.

3 Meanwhile, heat the oil in a skillet over medium-high heat. Add the onion and stir-fry 2 to 3 minutes until soft and translucent. Add the curry leaves, cumin, coriander, chili powder and turmeric, and stir-fry about 1 minute. Add the carrot and scallions and cook, stirring occasionally, 5 minutes, or until the carrots are tender. Add the ground beef and break up any lumps. Add 2 tablespoons water. Season with salt and pepper, then cook 5 to 7 minutes until cooked through, stirring occasionally. Stir in the mashed potatoes, then remove the pan from the heat and set aside.

4 Turn the dough onto a lightly oiled surface and knead for 5 minutes. Divide the dough into 14 portions and shape each into a ball. Brush the balls generously with oil, then place side by side on a well-oiled dish. Cover with plastic wrap and let stand at room temperature for 30 minutes.

5 Oil a clean work surface and generously oil your palms. Take a dough ball and flatten it, then slowly work the dough outward from around the edge until the circle is about 5½ or 6¼ inches in diameter. Place 2 tablespoons of the potato mixture in the center of the pastry, slightly flatten the mixture and mold into an oblong shape a generous ½ inch thick. Fold the bottom edge of the pastry over the filling, fold in the two sides and roll up tightly. Transfer to a lightly oiled plate and repeat until all the dough balls are used.

6 Lightly oil a large, nonstick skillet and place over medium-high heat. Fry 4 or 5 rotis at a time 8 to 10 minutes until crisp and brown all around, then turn the rotis upright and fry each end 2 to 3 minutes until brown spots form. Remove from the pan and keep warm. Repeat until all the rotis are cooked, then serve hot with chili sauce on the side, if liked.

sri Lankan crispy pancakes

Hoppers, also known as Appam, are crispy pancakes served in Sri Lanka at breakfast, lunch and dinner. They are cooked in a special pan that looks like a miniature wok, which gives the pancakes a curved shape when cooked. If you don't have a hopper pan, you can use either a small nonstick skillet or the bottom of a wok. Hoppers can be made in a variety of ways, both sweet and savory, and the egg hopper is one very popular example. Here I have included a recipe for a plain hopper, but I have included instructions on how to make simple sweet hoppers and egg hoppers, too. Because of their simple flavor and crisp outer layer, plain hoppers are great with curries.

MAKES 12
PREPARATION TIME 10 minutes, plus 2 hours resting time
COOKING TIME about 1 hour

PLAIN HOPPERS
2 teaspoons sugar
½ teaspoon sea salt
2¼ teaspoons active dry yeast granules
2 cups coconut milk
2 cups rice flour
2 eggs
sunflower oil, for oiling

SWEET HOPPERS
granulated or soft light brown sugar, to taste
shredded fresh coconut or dry unsweetened shredded coconut, to taste

EGG HOPPERS
12 eggs

1 Mix the sugar, salt and yeast in the coconut milk until dissolved. Put the rice flour in a large mixing bowl, make a well in the center and crack the eggs into the well. Gradually add the coconut milk mixture, whisking continuously to form a smooth batter. Cover with plastic wrap and let stand in a warm place 2 hours.

2 Pour some oil into a hopper pan or a 6¼-inch heavy-bottomed skillet over medium-high heat, then use paper towels to grease the pan evenly and soak up any excess oil. When the pan is hot, ladle about ⅓ cup of the batter into the center of the pan and quickly lift and swirl the pan to form a thin layer over the base and as far up the sides of the pan as possible to create a bowl shape. Cover the pan, reduce the heat to medium and cook 3 to 4 minutes until the edges begin to brown and bubbles start to form on the surface. The pancake should be crisp on the outside and slightly spongy in the middle. Transfer the hopper to a serving plate and keep warm, then repeat until all the batter is used.

3 To make sweet hoppers, sprinkle the plain hopper with sugar and coconut, to taste, halfway through cooking. Serve immediately.

4 To make egg hoppers, crack an egg into the center of each hopper after 1 to 2 minutes of cooking or when the batter starts to thicken and set. Continue to cook, still covered, to 2 minutes until the egg white turns solid and opaque. Serve immediately.

Basic Recipes

Within the main recipes you will often find references to spice pastes, condiments, rice and noodles, which will be either a key part of the recipe or a suggested accompaniment to the dish. All the recipes, including my foolproof method for boiling rice, can be found here. Each paste recipe makes the exact quantity you will need for the recipe, and takes 5 to 10 minutes to make, plus any soaking time required. You can use a mortar and pestle instead of a food processor to blend the pastes, if you prefer.

SPICE PASTES

Assam Laksa Spice Paste

4 dried chilies • 6 red chilies, seeded and roughly chopped • 1 teaspoon roasted shrimp paste (*see page 217*) • 10 shallots, roughly chopped • 1 lemongrass stalk, outer leaves and stalk end discarded, roughly chopped

1 Soak the dried chilies in hot water 10 minutes, then drain, seed and roughly chop. Put all the ingredients in a food processor and blend to a smooth paste.

Ayam Masak Merah Spice Paste

3 dried chilies • 10 shallots, roughly chopped • 4 garlic cloves, roughly chopped • ¾-inch piece of ginger root, peeled and roughly chopped • 3 red chilies, seeded and roughly chopped

1 Soak the dried chilies in hot water 10 minutes, then drain, seed and roughly chop. Put all the ingredients in a food processor and blend to a smooth paste.

Chili Crab Spice Paste

2 dried chilies • 5 red chilies, seeded and roughly chopped • 2 garlic cloves, roughly chopped • 6 shallots, roughly chopped • 2-inch piece of ginger-root, peeled and roughly chopped • 1 teaspoon roasted shrimp paste (*see page 217*)

1 Soak the dried chilies in hot water 10 minutes, then drain, seed and roughly chop. Put all the ingredients in a food processor and blend to a smooth paste.

Coorg-Style Curry Spice Paste

2 green chilies, seeded and roughly chopped • 1 red onion, roughly chopped • 3 garlic cloves, roughly chopped • ½-inch piece of ginger-root, peeled and roughly chopped • ¼ teaspoon black peppercorns • ½ teaspoon ground cumin • 1 teaspoon ground coriander

1 Put all the ingredients, except the cumin and coriander, in a food processor and blend to a smooth paste. Add the cumin and coriander and mix well.

COTO MAKASSAR SPICE PASTE

3 green chilies, seeded and roughly chopped • 2 red chilies, seeded and roughly chopped • 1¼-inch piece of ginger-root, peeled and roughly chopped • 3 garlic cloves, roughly chopped • 1⅔ cups cilantro leaves, roughly chopped • 1 teaspoon ground coriander • ½ teaspoon ground turmeric

1 Put all the ingredients, except the ground coriander and turmeric, in a food processor and blend to a smooth paste. Add the coriander and turmeric and mix well.

CURRY FISH MOUSSE SPICE PASTE

1 red chili, seeded and roughly chopped • 2 garlic cloves, roughly chopped • 5 shallots, roughly chopped • 2 lemongrass stalks, outer leaves and stalk ends discarded, roughly chopped • ½-inch piece of fresh turmeric, peeled and roughly chopped, or ½ teaspoon ground turmeric • ¾-inch piece of galangal, peeled and roughly chopped • 2 fresh lime leaves, roughly chopped

1 Put all the ingredients, except the ground turmeric, if using, in a food processor and blend to a smooth paste. Add the ground turmeric and mix well.

EGGPLANT CURRY SPICE PASTE

3 dried chilies • 2 red chilies, seeded and roughly chopped • 3 garlic cloves, roughly chopped • 5 shallots, roughly chopped • ½-inch piece of ginger-root, peeled and roughly chopped • ¼ teaspoon turmeric • ½ teaspoon ground coriander • ½ teaspoon ground cumin

1 Soak the dried chilies in hot water 10 minutes, then drain, seed and roughly chop. Put all the chilies, garlic, shallots and ginger in a food processor and blend into a smooth paste. Add the turmeric, coriander and cumin and mix well.

GADO GADO SPICE PASTE

3 red chilies, seeded and roughly chopped • 3 garlic cloves, roughly chopped • 5 shallots, roughly chopped • ¾-inch piece of ginger root, peeled and roughly chopped • 1 lemongrass stalk, outer leaves and stalk end discarded, roughly chopped • 1 tablespoon roasted shrimp paste (*see page 217*)

1 Blend all the ingredients in a food processor to a smooth paste.

KARE KARE SPICE PASTE

2 red chilies, seeded and roughly chopped • 4 garlic cloves, roughly chopped • 8 shallots, roughly chopped • ¾-inch piece of ginger root, peeled and roughly chopped • 1 teaspoon roasted shrimp paste (*see page 217*)

1 Blend all the ingredients in a food processor to a smooth paste.

KHMER YELLOW CURRY SPICE PASTE

1 red chili, seeded and roughly chopped • 4 garlic cloves, roughly chopped • 5 shallots, roughly chopped • 2 lemongrass stalks, outer leaves and stalk ends discarded, roughly chopped • 3 fresh lime leaves, roughly chopped • ¾-inch piece of galangal, peeled and roughly chopped • ¾-inch piece of fresh turmeric, peeled and roughly chopped, or 1 teaspoon ground turmeric

1 Put all the ingredients, except the ground turmeric, if using, in a food processor. Blend to a smooth paste. Add the ground turmeric and mix well.

LAKSA SPICE PASTE

10 dried chilies • 5 red chilies, seeded and roughly chopped • 6 garlic cloves, roughly chopped • 18 shallots, roughly chopped • 1 lemongrass stalk, outer leaves and stalk end discarded, roughly chopped • ¾-inch piece of ginger-root, peeled and roughly chopped • 1 tsp roasted shrimp paste (*see page 217*) • 2 macadamia nuts • 1½-inch piece of fresh turmeric, peeled and roughly chopped, or 2 teaspoon ground turmeric • 1 tablespoon ground coriander • 1 teaspoon ground cumin

1 Soak the dried chilies in hot water 10 minutes, then drain, seed and roughly chop. Put all the ingredients, except the ground turmeric, if using, coriander and cumin, in a food processor and blend to a smooth paste. Add the turmeric, ground coriander and cumin and mix well.

PAJERI NANAS SPICE PASTE

3 dried chilies • 6 red chilies, seeded and roughly chopped • 3 garlic cloves, roughly chopped • 10 shallots, roughly chopped • ½-inch piece of ginger-root, peeled and roughly chopped

1 Soak the dried chilies in hot water 10 minutes, then drain, seed and roughly chop. Put all the ingredients in a food processor and blend to a smooth paste.

PANANG CURRY SPICE PASTE

8 dried chilies • 2 red chilies, seeded and roughly chopped • 1 teaspoon roasted shrimp paste (*see page 217*) • 2 garlic cloves, roughly chopped • 4 shallots, roughly chopped • 1 lemongrass stalk, outer leaves and stalk end discarded, roughly chopped • 1¼-inch piece of galangal, peeled and roughly chopped • 2 fresh lime leaves, roughly chopped • 2 cilantro roots with stalks, roughly chopped • 1 teaspoon ground coriander • ½ teaspoon ground cumin

1 Soak the dried chilies in hot water 10 minutes, then drain, seed and roughly chop. Put all the ingredients, except the ground coriander and cumin, in a food processor and blend to a smooth paste. Add the coriander and cumin to the paste and mix well.

rendang spice paste

8 dried chilies • 4 red chilies, seeded and roughly chopped • 5 garlic cloves, roughly chopped • 1 red onion, roughly chopped • 10 shallots, roughly chopped • 1 lemongrass stalk, outer leaves and stalk end discarded, roughly chopped • ¾-inch piece of ginger root, peeled and roughly chopped • ¾-inch piece of galangal, peeled and roughly chopped • ¾-inch piece of fresh turmeric, peeled and roughly chopped, or 1 tsp ground turmeric • 1 tablespoon ground coriander • 1 teaspoon ground cumin

1 Soak the dried chilies in hot water 10 minutes, then drain, seed and roughly chop. Put all the ingredients, except the ground turmeric, if using, coriander and cumin, in a food processor and blend to a smooth paste. Add the ground turmeric, coriander and cumin and mix well.

sate lilit ikan spice paste

5 red chilies, seeded and roughly chopped • 4 garlic cloves, roughly chopped • 8 shallots, roughly chopped • 1¼-inch piece of ginger-root, peeled and roughly chopped • 1 lemongrass stalk, outer leaves and stalk end discarded, roughly chopped • 3 fresh lime leaves, roughly chopped • 2 macadamia nuts • 1 teaspoon roasted shrimp paste (*see page 217*) • ½-inch piece of fresh turmeric, peeled and roughly chopped, or ½ tsp ground turmeric • 1 teaspoon ground coriander

1 Put all the ingredients, except the ground turmeric, if using, and coriander in a food processor and blend to a smooth paste. Add the ground turmeric and coriander and mix well.

sour fish curry spice paste

½ teaspoon turmeric • ½ teaspoon ground coriander • ½ teaspoon chili powder • ¼ teaspoon ground cumin • ¼ teaspoon freshly ground black pepper • 3 shallots, roughly chopped • 2 garlic cloves, roughly chopped • 3 green chilies, seeded and roughly chopped • ½-inch piece of ginger root, peeled and roughly chopped

1 Put the turmeric, coriander, chili powder, cumin and black pepper in a skillet over medium-high heat and dry-fry 1 to 2 minutes until fragrant and slightly smoky. Transfer to a mixing bowl. Put the shallots, garlic, green chilies and ginger in a food processor and blend to a smooth paste. Add the toasted spice powder and mix well.

squid spice paste

4 dried chilies • 5 red chilies, seeded and roughly chopped • 3 garlic cloves, roughly chopped • 10 shallots, roughly chopped • 1 tsp roasted shrimp paste (*see page 217*) • 2 macadamia nuts

1 Soak the dried chilies in hot water 10 minutes, then drain, seed and roughly chop. Put all the ingredients in a food processor and blend to a smooth paste.

THAI GREEN CURRY SPICE PASTE

7 green chilies, seeded and roughly chopped • 2 red bird's-eye chilies, seeded and roughly chopped • 5 shallots, roughly chopped • 3 garlic cloves, roughly chopped • 1¼-inch piece of galangal, peeled and roughly chopped • 1 lemongrass stalk, outer leaves and stalk end discarded, roughly chopped • 3 fresh lime leaves, roughly chopped • 1 teaspoon roasted shrimp paste (*see page 217*) • 3 cilantro roots with stalks and leaves, roughly chopped • ¼-inch piece of fresh turmeric, peeled and chopped, or ¼ teaspoon ground turmeric

1 Put all the ingredients, except the ground turmeric, if using, in a food processor. Blend to a smooth paste. Add the ground turmeric and mix well.

THAI RED CURRY SPICE PASTE

8 dried chilies • 2 red chilies, seeded and roughly chopped • 2 garlic cloves, roughly chopped • 4 shallots, roughly chopped • ½ lemongrass stalk, outer leaves and stalk end discarded, roughly chopped • 1¼-inch piece of galangal, peeled and roughly chopped • 1 tsp roasted shrimp paste (*see page 217*) • 2 cilantro roots with stalks, roughly chopped • 2 fresh lime leaves, roughly chopped

1 Soak the dried chilies in hot water 10 minutes, then drain, seed and roughly chop. Put all the ingredients in a food processor and blend to a smooth paste.

THAI ROAST CHICKEN SPICE PASTE

1 red chili, seeded and roughly chopped • 3 shallots, roughly chopped • 1 lemongrass stalk, outer leaves and stalk end removed, roughly chopped • 2 cilantro roots with stalks, roughly chopped • ¾-inch piece of fresh turmeric, peeled and roughly chopped, or 1 teaspoon ground turmeric

1 Put all the ingredients, except the ground turmeric, if using, in a food processor. Blend to a smooth paste. Add the ground turmeric and mix well.

STOCKS

CHICKEN STOCK

1 pound 12 ounces chicken wings and drumsticks, skin and excess fat removed, or 3-pound 4-ounce chicken carcass • 2-inch piece of ginger-root, peeled and finely chopped • 6 scallions, cut in half lengthwise • 5 garlic cloves, chopped • ¼ teaspoon white peppercorns • 1 star anise • 2 tablespoons Shaoxing rice wine

1 Put the chicken, ginger, scallions, garlic, white peppercorns, star anise and rice wine in a large saucepan over medium-high heat. Add 2 quarts water and bring to a boil. Reduce the heat to low, cover and simmer 2 to 3 hours, skimming off any scum from the surface as required.
2 Remove the pan from the heat and discard all the solid ingredients. Cool the stock, then strain over a bowl lined with cheesecloth. Chicken stock can be frozen up to 1 month.

POrK STOCK

10½ ounces chicken wings and drumsticks, skin and excess fat removed
• 1 pound 2 ounces pork ribs or pork bones • 2-inch piece of ginger-root,
peeled and finely chopped • 3 scallions, cut in half lengthwise • 5 garlic cloves,
finely chopped • ¼ teaspoon white peppercorns

1 Put the chicken pieces, pork ribs, ginger, scallions, garlic, white
  peppercorns and 2 quarts water in a large saucepan and bring to a boil.
  Reduce the heat to low and simmer 2 to 3 hours, skimming off any scum
  from the surface as required.
2 Remove the pan from the heat and discard all the solid ingredients. Cool
  the stock, then strain over a bowl lined with cheesecloth. Pork stock can
  be frozen up to 1 month.

DaSHI

4½-inch piece kombu • 1 ounce dried bonito flakes

1 Wipe the kombu with damp paper towels to remove any powder residue.
  Put the kombu in a saucepan and add 5 cups water. Let sit 30 minutes.
  Place the saucepan over medium-low heat, bring to a boil and then
  remove the kombu. Reduce the heat to low, add the bonito flakes, cover
  and simmer about 5 minutes.
2 Remove the pan from the heat and let the bonito flakes sink to the
  bottom. Skim off any scum from the surface, then strain the stock over
  a bowl lined with cheesecloth. Leave the dashi to cool. This is Ichiban
  Dashi, which is the first stock with a more intense flavor.
3 You can reuse the kombu and bonito flakes to make Niban Dashi, which
  is the second stock with a milder flavor. Use the same amount of water as
  above and simmer all the ingredients about 10 minutes. Strain the stock
  through cheesecloth as above and discard the solids. Dashi can be frozen
  up to 1 month.

CONDIMENTS & SIDES

CHILI OIL

scant 1¼ cups sunflower oil • cinnamon stick, 2-inch • 1 star anise
• ¾ cup dried red pepper flakes • 1 teaspoon Sichuan peppercorns, crushed

1 Heat the oil in a deep, heavy-bottomed skillet to about 315°F, or until a
  small piece of bread dropped into the oil turns brown after 25 to 30
  seconds. Add the cinnamon stick and star anise and fry 1 to 2 minutes,
  stirring occasionally, until fragrant. Discard the cinnamon stick and star
  anise.
2 Make sure the oil is still hot, but no hotter, and add the dried red pepper
  flakes. Stir a few seconds, then remove the pan from the heat.
3 Leave the oil and dried red pepper flakes to cool and then transfer to
  a sterilized preserving jar or bottle. The chili oil can be kept in the
  refrigerator sealed in a jar for many weeks.

CHILI Paste

½ cup (about 1¾ ounces) dried chilies • 3 tablespoons sunflower oil •1 tablespoon sugar • ½ teaspoon salt

1 Soak the dried chilies in hot water 10 to 15 minutes, then drain, seed and roughly chop. Put the chilies in a food processor and blend to a smooth paste.
2 Heat the oil in a skillet over medium-high heat. Add the chili paste and cook gently, stirring occasionally, for 15 to 20 minutes until fragrant and the oil starts to rise to the surface. Stir in the sugar and salt, remove from the heat and cool. Chili paste can be frozen for up to 2 months.

FrIeD SHALLOTS

1 cup sunflower oil • ¾ pound red shallots, thinly sliced

1 Heat the oil in a skillet over medium heat. Insert a chopstick into the oil. When bubbles will start to form around the chopstick the oil is ready to use. Add the shallots and fry, stirring occasionally, about 5 to 7 minutes until golden brown. Using a slotted spoon, remove the shallots from the pan and drain in a fine sieve over a mixing bowl, then on paper towels to soak up any excess oil.
2 Reuse the oil for cooking, if liked. Cool, then store in an airtight container in a cool, dark place for later use up to 1 week.

Ground Toasted Sichuan Pepper

¼ cup Sichuan peppercorns

1 Heat a skillet over medium-low heat. Add the Sichuan peppercorns and dry-fry 5 minutes, or until fragrant, but don't allow them to burn.
2 Remove from the heat and let cool. Grind the peppercorns in a food processor or coffee grinder and store in a cool, dark place in an airtight jar up to 1 month.

Nam PrIK Pao

½ cup (about 1¾ ounces) dried chilies, rinsed • 1 ounce dried shrimp, rinsed • ½ cup sunflower oil • 6 medium garlic cloves, sliced • 3½ ounces shallots, sliced • 1 teaspoon roasted shrimp paste (*see page 217*) • 2 tablespoon fish sauce • 1 recipe quantity Tamarind Water (*see page 217*)

1 Heat a skillet over medium-high heat. Add the dried chilies and dry-fry 2 to 3 minutes until slightly smoky. Remove from the pan. Set aside. Make sure your kitchen is well ventilated because the smell can be strong.
2 Using the same pan, lightly fry the dried shrimp 2 to 3 minutes until fragrant and the color changes. Set aside to cool.
3 Meanwhile, heat the oil in a deep skillet or wok over medium heat. Add the garlic and shallots and fry, stirring occasionally, 5 to 7 minutes until lightly golden brown. Using a slotted spoon, remove the shallots and garlic from the oil. Set aside the skillet, with the oil, for later use.
4 Once the shallots and garlic are cool, put in a food processor with the dried chilies, toasted dried shrimps and roasted shrimp paste, and blend to a slightly coarse paste.

5 Reheat the oil in the skillet over medium-low heat. Add the chili paste and cook gently, stirring occasionally, for 5 minutes, or until fragrant and the color has darkened. Mix in the fish sauce and tamarind water. Transfer the paste to a preserving jar and cool. Store in the refrigerator for up to 1 month.

NUOC CHAM DIPPING sauce

1 garlic clove, finely chopped • 1 teaspoon chopped red bird's-eye chili • 2 tablespoons sugar • 5 tablespoons lime juice • 2 tablespoons fish sauce

1 Put all the ingredients in a bowl, add 2 tablespoons water and stir until the sugar has dissolved.

PICKLED ginger

1 pound 2 ounces ginger-root • 1 tablespoon salt • scant 1½ cups rice vinegar • scant 1¼ cups sugar

1 Cut the ginger into small pieces for easier handling. Hold the ginger firmly in one hand and scrape off the peel using a spoon or a small, sharp knife. Cut the ginger into slices about 1/16 inch thick.
2 Put the ginger in a colander and rub with the salt to draw out the moisture. Let sit in the colander about 1 hour, then rinse thoroughly under cold running water. Squeeze out any excess liquid and pat dry with paper towels. Transfer the ginger to a large preserving jar.
3 Put the rice vinegar and sugar in a saucepan over medium-high heat. Bring to a boil, stirring continuously until the sugar has dissolved. Pour the liquid over the ginger and let to cool.
4 Cover and refrigerate 24 to 36 hours before using. Pickled ginger can be stored in the fridge up to 1 month.

SAMBAL

2 teaspoons roasted shrimp paste (*see page 217*) • 5 red chilies, seeded and roughly chopped • 3 green bird's-eye chilies, seeded and roughly chopped • 2 teaspoons sugar • juice of 1 lime • ¼ teaspoon salt

1 Put the roasted shrimp paste and chilies in a food processor and blend to a smooth paste. Transfer to a mixing bowl, add the sugar, lime juice and salt, and stir until the sugar is dissolved. Store in a preserving jar in the refrigerator up to 1 week.

SAMBAL MATAH

1 teaspoon roasted shrimp paste (*see page 217*) • 5 shallots, finely sliced • 2 garlic cloves, finely chopped • 2 red bird's-eye chilies, seeded and finely chopped • 2 fresh lime leaves, finely chopped • 2 teaspoons sugar • 2 tablespoons lime juice • a pinch of salt

1 Put all the ingredients in a bowl and mix until the sugar has dissolved and the paste well combined.

RICE

BOILED RICE

heaping 1⅓ cups short-grain rice or 1¾ cups long-grain rice, such as jasmine and basmati

1 Put the rice in a large saucepan and pour in enough water to half fill the pan. Swirl the rice using your hand, lightly rubbing the grains, until the water is cloudy. Carefully pour off the water and repeat this process 3 or 4 times until the water is almost clear.

**For Boiled
Short-Grain Rice**

2 Drain the rice into a strainer and let sit over a bowl about 10 minutes, then transfer the rice to the saucepan and add scant 1½ cups water. Set aside about 20 minutes, then bring to a boil over high heat and give it a quick stir. Reduce the heat to low, cover with a tight-fitting lid and simmer gently about 15 minutes, or until the liquid has been absorbed.

3 Remove the pan from the heat and then, using a wooden or plastic spatula, quickly loosen the grains. Replace the lid and leave the rice to steam 15 minutes until fluffy.

**For Boiled
Long-Grain Rice**

2 Cover the rice with water and let stand 30 minutes. Drain the rice into a strainer and let sit over a bowl 10 minutes, then transfer the rice to a saucepan and add scant 2 cups water. Place the pan over high heat and bring to a boil about 20 seconds. Stir the rice with a wooden spoon to prevent from sticking to the bottom of the pan. Reduce the heat to low, cover and simmer gently 20 minutes.

3 Remove the pan from the heat, leaving the lid tightly closed, and set aside to steam 10 to 15 minutes until the rice is cooked. Fluff the rice with a fork and keep warm.

BASIC TECHNIQUES

cooking egg and rice noodles and rice sticks

1 Prepare a large bowl of ice-cold water and place it next to the stove. Fill a large saucepan with plenty of water and bring to a boil, then add the noodles or rice sticks and cook for the following times:

Fresh egg noodles   blanch 25 to 30 seconds to warm through

Dried egg noodles   cook 3 to 4 minutes until "al dente"

Rice sticks   cook 2 to 3 minutes until "al dente"

Dried rice vermicelli   cook 2 to 3 minutes until "al dente"

Thick rice noodles   soak in boiling water 30 to 45 minutes, then cook 4 to 5 minutes until "al dente"

2 Using a noodle skimmer or long-handled tongs, remove the cooked noodles from the water and plunge a few seconds into the ice-cold water. Meanwhile, bring the water in the pan back to a boil. Return the noodles to the boiling water a few seconds to warm through, then drain and continue according to the recipe instructions.

cooking soba noodles

1 Bring plenty of water to a boil in a large saucepan, add the soba noodles and cook about 3 to 4 minutes or until al dente. If unsure if they are ready, take a bite from a strand of noodle—it should be cooked through completely without a hard core.
2 Drain the noodles and rinse under cold running water, swirling and gently rubbing the strands to remove the starch. Continue rinsing until the water runs clear.
3 Meanwhile, bring another saucepan of water to a boil. Plunge the cooked and rinsed soba noodles into the water for a few seconds to heat through, then drain and continue according to the recipe instructions.

deboning chicken legs

1 Rinse the chicken legs under cold running water and pat dry with paper towels. Place one leg, skin-side down, on a cutting board and cut through the joint between the thigh and the drumstick using a large, sharp knife.
2 Take the thigh and make an incision along the top of the bone. Using quick, short strokes, deepen the incision to cut the meat away from the bone. Pull clear the top part of the bone and then continue to make a few more cuts to remove the bone completely. Cut off any small bits of bone, tendons, fat and skin.
3 Use the same process to remove the bone from the drumstick. Repeat for the remaining legs.

Freshly grated coconut

1 Insert a sharp metal skewer into the "eyes" at the bottom of the coconut and drain out the juice. Heat the oven to 350°F and bake the coconut about 15 minutes. Remove from the oven and set aside until cool enough to handle.

2 Using a hammer or cleaver, tap the middle of the coconut until cracks form, then break the coconut in two. If you have a coconut grater, use it to grate the coconut. If not, carefully slip a small, sharp knife between the shell and the flesh and pull the flesh away. Peel the brown skin off the back of the flesh using a vegetable peeler, then cut the flesh in chunks. Grate the flesh using a hand-held grater or blend it in a food processor to a shredded-coconut consistency.

Fresh coconut milk

1 Grate the flesh, as above, and mix with scant 1 cup water. Strain over a bowl lined with cheesecloth, squeezing out as much milk as possible. This is the "first press". It is thick and concentrated and is sometimes known as coconut cream. Set the milk aside while you extract the "second press" coconut milk.

2 Add 3 tablespoons water to the grated coconut in the cheesecloth and strain over a separate bowl, squeezing out as much milk as possible. It will have a much thinner consistency.

3 Unless a recipe specifically asks for coconut cream or second-press coconut milk, blend both the first- and second-press milks together. Coconut milk can be prepared in advance and can be frozen up to 6 months.

Preparing shrimp

1 Hold the body of the shrimp firmly, squeeze and pull off the head. Peel away the shell and legs from the body then, holding the body, squeeze off the tail. Reserve the shell and head if using in a recipe or reserve them to flavor a stock.

2 To devein the shrimp, hold it so the back of the shrimp is slightly curved. Using a small knife, make a shallow incision along the back. Use a toothpick to remove the black vein.

3 If the shrimp are to be used whole, make a few incisions vertically along the belly. This will prevent it from curling up during cooking.

4 Rinse the shrimp in cold, running water and drain. Transfer the shrimp to a deep bowl, add 1 tablespoon sea salt and use your hands to lightly massage the salt into the shrimp. (Salt is used at this stage is to give the shrimp a springy texture.) Rinse the shrimp under cold running water, drain and pat dry with paper towels.

Preparing squid

1 Place the squid on a cutting board and spread the tentacles out on the board. Cut off and discard the two longest tentacles.

2 Take the head in one hand and the body in the other and gently pull the head away from the body. The head will take the intestines with it. Cut just in front of the eyes and remove and discard the eyes and intestines.

3 Next, pull out and discard the inedible beak from the base of the tentacles and the transparent silver quill found inside the body.

4 Finally, pull off the two fins on either side of the body and pull away the spotted skin from both the body and the fins. Discard the fins and use the tentacles, if liked. Thoroughly rinse the pieces of squid, inside and out, under cold running water, then pat dry with paper towels.

5 Squid can be cut into rings or scored with a diamond pattern. To do this, cut open the body by sliding a sharp, flexible knife into the opening of the body and along its entire length. Flatten the body out on a cutting board, inner surface facing up. Position your knife at 90° to the surface, then make very shallow diagonal crisscross cuts into the flesh. Scoring the squid on the inside surface makes it curl with the inside facing out when cooked. Cut the body into pieces according to the recipe instructions.

PREPARING BEEF TO BE THINLY SLICED

1 Rinse the beef under cold running water and pat dry with paper towels. Cover with plastic wrap and freeze about 25 minutes, or until the beef is firm to the touch but not frozen solid.

2 Remove the beef from the freezer, discard the plastic wrap and place the beef on a cutting board. Using a sharp knife, cut the beef against the grain into ⅛-inch slices, or even thinner if possible.

REHYDRATING DRIED MUSHROOMS

1 Put the dried mushrooms in a bowl. Pour over boiling water to cover and soak 20 to 25 minutes until soft. Strain the liquid into another bowl, if using, squeezing any excess liquid from the mushrooms. Cut off the stems.

ROASTED SHRIMP PASTE

1 Put the recipe quantity of shrimp paste in the middle of a square piece of foil and break it into pieces with a spoon. Fold in the edges of the foil to form a small package. Roast in a preheated oven at 400°F about 5 minutes. Remove and set aside to cool. The roasted shrimp will smell aromatic and darken into dry powder.

SKINNING TOMATOES

1 Score the base of the tomato, put in a bowl and cover with boiling water. Let stand until the skin starts to curl. Drain off the hot water then fill the bowl with cold water. Let cool, strain, and remove the skins.

TAMARIND WATER

1 Put 1¾ ounces tamarind pulp and ⅓ cup boiling water in a small bowl. Let soak 30 minutes or until soft. Use the back of a spoon to break up the pulp, then pour the liquid through a fine strainer set over a bowl. Discard the solids.

TOASTED DRIED ANCHOVIES

1 Remove the heads and guts from the dried anchovies, then rinse under cold running water, drain and pat dry with paper towels.

2 Heat 1 teaspoon vegetable oil in a skillet over medium heat. Add the anchovies and toast until they turn golden brown.

glossary

BEAN CURD SHEET This is made from the layer of film that forms on the surface of soymilk when it is made. The film is collected and dried until it becomes a translucent sheet.

BLACK BEAN PASTE Made from fermented and salted soybeans and with a pungent smell and bittersweet taste, black bean paste is often used in stir-fries.

BONITO FLAKES, DRIED Known as katsuobushi in Japanese, bonito flakes are dried, fermented and smoked skipjack tuna shavings. They are commonly used in making dashi stock and miso soup.

CHILI BEAN PASTE Also known as dou ban jiang in Mandarin Chinese. Chili bean paste is made of chili pepper, fermented soybeans, fermented fava beans and a mixture of spices. It tastes both slightly spicy and salty at the same time.

CHINESE BLACK RICE VINEGAR Sometimes called Chinkiang vinegar, after the place from where it is produced, this vinegar tastes very similar to balsamic vinegar. It is often used in dipping sauces and in stir-fries.

CHINESE FIVE-SPICE This is a mix of five spices including black peppercorns, cloves, cinnamon, fennel seed and star anise. It is used in braised dishes and also to marinate meat. Ready-ground powder is widely available in the supermarket.

DAIKON Also known as Chinese radish, or mooli in India, daikon is shaped like a very long carrot. It has a mild flavor and is often used in Japanese stews and as a pickled condiment.

DRIED ANCHOVIES These are the small, saltwater fish that have been dried. Dried anchovies are often used in Korean cuisine as a stock base and commonly feature in Sambal dishes of Malaysia and Indonesia. Most of the time, however, they are fried until crisp in texture and then added to salads or fried rice.

GALANGAL A rhizome from the ginger family, it has a pale yellow and pinkish skin and citrusy flavor. Galangal is normally used in curry pastes or to infuse stock.

GLUTINOUS RICE A type of short-grain rice that is normally soaked before steaming and becomes very sticky once cooked. It is sometimes called sticky rice.

GLUTINOUS RICE FLOUR A highly absorbent flour made from glutinous rice. Often used in Asian desserts, it becomes sticky, rubbery and chewy in texture.

HOISIN SAUCE Commonly used as a condiment, it has a thick, sticky texture and is brown in color. Hoisin sauce is made from soybeans, vinegar, sugar and other spices. The sweet, garlicky flavor of hoisin sauce makes it a popular ingredient in marinades.

JAGGERY Widely used in Asian cooking, jaggery is obtained from the sugary sap of certain palm trees. It usually comes in blocks, which you can chop or slice, but is also found in granular and liquid form. If not available, replace with soft light brown sugar.

JERUSALEM ARTICHOKES Not related to the artichoke family, despite the name, the Jerusalem artichoke is a root vegetable that looks very like ginger-root. It has a sweet and nutty flavor and a crisp, crunchy texture, and can be eaten either raw or cooked.

JICAMA Also known as yam bean, jicama is a root vegetable commonly used in Southeast Asian and Central American cooking. It has a similar shape to the white round radish but is bigger. Jicama has a crunchy texture and can be eaten raw and cooked. Substitutes for jicama are Jerusalem artichokes and water chestnuts.

KOMBU, DRIED An edible kelp that is widely used in Japanese cooking and, in the dried form, is one of the main ingredients in dashi. It is also sold pickled.

KOREAN RED PEPPER POWDER Called kochukara in Korea, this is a powder form of Korean dried red pepper. Korean red pepper is another variety of red chili that is sun-dried. It is used in many Korean dishes, such as Kimchi and Bulgogi.

KOREAN HOT PEPPER PASTE Known as gochujang in Korea, this paste is salty, spicy and pungent. It is made from Korean dried red pepper, fermented soybeans and other spices. It is normally used as a condiment, marinade or seasoning, and is very similar to Chili Bean Paste.

LOTUS LEAVES As the name indicates, these come from the lotus plant and are used dried. The leaf is large and bright green in color. It is most often used as a receptacle to cook sticky rice and imparts a more earthy and smoky flavor as well as keeping the ingredients moist.

MIRIN A Japanese sweet rice wine with a low alcohol content, mirin has a strong flavor, is very sweet and is often used instead of sugar.

NORI A dried sheet of seaweed, nori is used to make sushi and sometimes forms a garnish. It is slightly salty in flavor and has a crisp texture.

PANDAN LEAVES Also known as screwpine leaves, pandan leaves are green, thin, long and pointed, and are used as a flavoring in savory dishes and as coloring in desserts. When used as a flavoring in stocks or rice, they are normally tied into a knot for easy removal. Alternatively, they can be snipped into pieces and then blended into a paste. The juice is then squeezed out and used. Pandan essence can be found at Asian supermarkets and is mostly used in making desserts.

SAGO PEARLS Sago is extracted from the pith of sago palm stems. They are very tiny and white. Sago pearls are commonly used in Southeast Asia in desserts, and when cooked turn translucent.

SAKE A popular alcoholic drink in Japan, sake is made from fermented rice. Because "drinking" sake is very expensive for use in cooking, there is a cheaper "cooking" variety available in Asian supermarkets.

SHOYU This is the Japanese version of light soy sauce but, compared to Chinese light soy sauce, it has a richer and stronger flavor. It is great in stir-fries, marinades or served as a condiment.

SHRIMP PASTE Shrimp paste is widely used in Southeast Asian cooking. It normally comes in a block and is made from fermented shrimp that has been dried in the sun. It is known as belacan in Malay, terasi in Indonesian, kapi in Thai and khmer mam ruoc in Vietnamese. Uncooked shrimp paste is a bit sticky and has a pungent and strong fishy smell. Because of this, it is not advisable to toast shrimp paste in a pan in your kitchen, but to roast it in the oven instead (*see page 217*).

SICHUAN PEPPERCORNS These peppercorns are reddish brown in color and have a unique and strong flavor. They are normally toasted before use in order to bring out the aroma.

TAMARIND PEEL This is sun-dried slices of the small, round, sour-tasting asam gelugor fruit grown on a tree native to Malaysia. It is also known as asam keping and not related to the tamarind fruit. Tamarind peel is mostly used in fish-based curries in Malaysia and Singapore.

TAMARIND PULP This is the sticky pulp taken from the inside of the tamarind pod. It is dark brown in color and is normally sold in a block. The pulp needs to be soaked in warm water for about 30 minutes before being used to make tamarind water (*see page 217*).

THAI BASIL The Thai basil leaf is long and pointed with a purple stem. It has a much stronger and more pungent flavor than sweet basil and is normally used in salads, stir-fries and curry dishes.

VIETNAMESE CILANTRO LEAVES This is the most common name for polygonum leaves and is also known as Vietnamese mint, as well as laksa leaves in Indonesia and daun kesom in Malaysia and Singapore. Vietnamese cilantro is normally used to infuse soup stock.

WAKAME Wakame is a long, deep-green seaweed that usually comes in a dried form. A popular ingredient in Japanese cuisine, it is commonly used in salads or added to miso soup. Dried wakame must be rehydrated in water before it can be used.

WATER CHESTNUT A small, round aquatic vegetable, water chestnuts can be eaten raw or cooked. The flesh has a crunchy texture.

WATER SPINACH Known as ong choi in China, this is a semiaquatic vegetable with long, pointed leaves and an extended, hollow stem. The texture is crunchy and it is normally used in stir-fries and soup dishes.

WASABI Also known as Japanese horseradish, wasabi has a very strong, fiery flavor. Once eaten, it stimulates the nasal passage, unlike chili, which produces a hot sensation on the tongue. Wasabi is most commonly used as a condiment for sushi.

INDEX

AUTHOR ACKNOWLEDGMENTS

Thank you to...
Arnaud, for being so very patient and supportive throughout the period that this book was being written. It wouldn't have been the same without your feedback when I was testing the recipes.
Mom and Dad, for bringing me into this world and for all your guidance and advice all these years.
My sister, for all of your great effort in helping me to test and retest the recipes. I wouldn't have been able to make it without your help.
My brother, for loving my food since you were little.
Nelly, for your support and testing some of the recipes. You have inspired me!
Azma, for being a great friend and for helping with the recipe testing. You put a smile on my face when you said, "It's very delicious!"
Kristin, I finally managed to get you to cook and I hope this is just the beginning of the journey.
Grace, for your patience, guidance and support. It has been a great pleasure to know you. Thank you for giving me this amazing opportunity to author this book!
Camilla, for your great work in editing this book. Your words of encouragement have given me even more confidence in and enthusiasm for writing!
The loyal readers of my blog, My Cooking Hut, for your readership, support and words of encouragement.

Thank you, Lord, for being my strength and guidance.

TEXTILE PHOTO CREDITS